CW01551182

Born in Germany to Italian parents, a turning point came in Ivana's life, when still in her teen years, half of her family tragically lost their lives. The immense stress and pain caused by this tragedy, compelled Ivana to question her existence. Curiosity took Ivana on a quest to explore universal knowledge and experiment with the extraordinary, leading her to discovering the unimaginable powers that humans can harness, leading to portals to other worlds.

'What I had lived through was so far from ordinary, so far from mundane that at the time it seemed surreal. My deep curiosity brought me to discover a fuller story about myself, of this broader being that was more than this one character that I was playing in this one lifetime.'

Now based in Kensington, London, Ivana believes that we are all multi-talented and that there are no limits to what we can achieve. Influenced by diversity, Ivana likes her life to be a life of constant growth and positive changes. The story in this book is Ivana's story, Ivana is an individual with a great desire to inspire and uplift.

The aim of this collection of words is to remind you of how beautiful and powerful you all are and worthy of the very best that life has to offer. To prompt all the creative people of this wonderful world, and those who believe in their own greatness but are still dreaming. Encouraging the artist and creators, old and young, those who desire to live life to the fullest, remember you are beautiful beings with superpowers and capable of the fulfilment of your deepest dreams no matter where you stand in your life.

"I am thankful for all the editing assistance I had throughout my life from software to humans, which assisted me in compiling my writing. And I feel grateful for having been able to put my thoughts onto paper turning them into this book, as there was once a time when I would have never believed that I would be capable of writing a book."

With Love
Ivana
WWW.IVANABASILOTTA.CO.UK

Dedicated to my friend,
Mike.
The one who knows me best.
My hero friend.

Ivana Basllotta

BRAINWASHED AND BACK

OWNING ME –

SECRETS I OWN

AUSTIN MACAULEY PUBLISHERS™

LONDON • CAMBRIDGE • NEW YORK • SHARJAH

Copyright © Ivana Basilotta 2024

The right of Ivana Basilotta to be identified as author of this work has been asserted by the author in accordance with sections 77 and 78 of the Copyright, Designs and Patents Act 1988.

All rights reserved. No part of this publication may be reproduced, stored in a retrieval system, or transmitted in any form or by any means, electronic, mechanical, photocopying, recording, or otherwise, without the prior permission of the publishers.

Any person who commits any unauthorised act in relation to this publication may be liable to criminal prosecution and civil claims for damages.

A CIP catalogue record for this title is available from the British Library.

ISBN 9781528974417 (Paperback)
ISBN 9781528974431 (ePub e-book)

www.austinmacauley.com

First Published 2024
Austin Macauley Publishers Ltd®
1 Canada Square
Canary Wharf
London
E14 5AA

Contents

Preface

'Science is more than a body of knowledge, it's a way of thinking. A way of sceptically interrogating the universe with a fine understanding of human fallibility. If we are not able to ask sceptical questions, to interrogate those who tell us that something is true, to be sceptical of those in authority, then we're up for grabs for the next charlatan, political or religious, who comes ambling along.'

Carl Sagan, in one of his final interviews.

Foreword

There are many things we can accomplish in life, even things we feel are impossible. In my third year of school, my German teacher prompted me to read a passage out of a book, before returning the results of my written test. I was about nine years old. I read the chapter out loud to the class and was called to the front immediately. As I nervously stood next to my teacher, I was handed my checked test papers that were full of mistakes. In a stern tone, my teacher turned around and launched a fist at my arm, announcing, 'I have never come across anyone that reads so well and writes so badly,' leaving me with a big bruise.

Since then, I have learned to speak three languages fluently but found myself making errors when writing in any of them. After all, I had been 'labelled.' Writing was not supposed to be my strength, but I have ended up writing a lot throughout my life, some of my articles even found their way into published media. I wrote for my work and kept a personal memoir. I developed a great joy for reading. Books have kept me inspired throughout my life, they have nurtured me, educated me and changed my world.

But it was a sentence I once read that encouraged me to write and made it okay for me to be imperfect. *'To err is human, to edit is divine.'*

You Are Wonderful

It was still dark when I awoke, laying serenely In my cosy double bed, at my London home, gazing at my bedroom ceiling. Looking up, I could see the bright stars sparkling through the ceiling of my bedroom. However strange it seemed to see those stars through the roof, as I drifted in and out of sleep, it felt like the most natural thing. The ceiling was still in place, it was as if some mysterious energy had transformed the way I could see. Inexplicably, I could adjust my sight to see through matter, my vision took me straight through the plaster of the ceiling and the timbers of the roof upwards into the night sky, where each star was brilliantly shining. I felt that the sparkling stars were alive and performing just for me, some of them moved close as if we shared a magnetic mutual attraction. Those shining stars were sitting on the rooftops and also around me, brightly illuminating the streets for me. Mesmerised by what I saw, I had to check that I was not dreaming. I forced my eyes wide open, my mind becoming crystal clear, so clear, that I could understand the meaning of everything that I was observing, perfectly coexisting within the universal laws that govern our cosmos. What I saw was magical and captivating, the Milky Way was perfectly aligned. I sensed the energy projected by each star and planet, a power that was keeping the Earth in perfect balance, like the sway of creation, I felt myself merging with this energy. I became the stars, and the stars became me, I felt perfectly in harmony.

Words that were not mine, started to flood into my mind in a whisper I heard, *'do not hold back, live your dreams, tap into your own magic. There is an imprint within you, an inner guide that will lead you to the fulfilment of your dreams. You hold the power to transform worlds and create a satisfying, purposeful life filled with wellbeing, creativity, good fortune, love, and happiness. Remain brave, it is never too late to fulfil your deepest desires. You are wonderful, and your opportunities are endless. Dare to live your dreams, as this is who you are meant to be.'*

It was still dawn when I stepped out of my bed and walked across the white wooden floors into my living room and towards the high floor to ceiling bay windows that overlooked the manicured gardens. I slid the window up wide open to glance at the vibrant Cornwall Gardens square that nestled within the graceful elevated white stucco fronted houses in the midst of South Kensington. A delicious fresh breeze moved through the space of the apartment as if to greet me, this morning my home looked particularly pretty, gleaming in white the whole room seemed illuminated, my living room, seemed brighter than usual. The white satin curtains hung gracefully down beside the tall windows, softly swaying in the mild breeze. I stood by the window gazing out into a serene space, still mesmerised by the experience I had while the rest of the world had been asleep. The stars had spoken to me. I could have sworn that it was not a dream.

Keep Your Dreams Close

A little girl secretly dreamed of becoming a heroic actress of the stage and screen. Mesmerised by each performance she saw, she imagined how much fun it would be to play the characters she had observed. She was often found pretending to be a newsreader, rehearsing a scene from a movie that she had just seen, or studying a glossy TV magazine, admiring the photographs of the movie stars in beautiful dresses that graced its pages. Though the little girl never spoke to anyone about her dreams, she had heard people say that actresses were discovered at a young age. She started to believe that this was the road to becoming a performing artist. She bided her time keeping her dreams close to her, in case she would be teased.

Unaware that dreams had the potential to turn into a reality, the little girl figured that if she could look like an actress, perhaps she would then be discovered. She had observed her mother creating garments on a sewing machine and she too wanted to own a uniquely bespoke wardrobe just like those starlets she had observed in the media. Her mother was very encouraging and supportive in showing and guiding her interests, inspired at just twelve years old, she had learned how to use a sewing machine and how to construct her own unique style in the process, she discovered a fondness, for textiles, draping them around her, creating patterns and garments and was forever busy making her masterpieces. It was the idea of being able to create things out of scrap that was most fascinating to her. Art and handicraft classes at school became favourites. She spent all her spare time refining her technique.

Two years later, her school introduced a video acting class. With great excitement she enrolled in the course and became one of the leading acts in the production. The amateur production team produced three films and even hosted a film premiere at her school. She wore an outfit that she had designed and created with her mother's help a pair of Reiter pants she had made from her mother's bed linen, combined with a blue blouse. Her photograph appeared on the front page of the local newspaper. She looked just like a movie star at only fourteen years old. In some way, her dream had come true.

Fast forward a few years and the girl was now a young woman. She had left her homeland Germany and moved to London for further studies. While living in London, she noticed the advertising cards of a local drama school that kept coming through her letterbox. Convinced she would never be accepted, she never took any action. Along the way, she had made a mistake, she had shared her secret aspiration to be an actress with a person who believed in limitations. That person had convincingly told her that she would never be accepted in any performing art schools with her German accent. So, the girl had started to doubt herself and her ability to fulfil her dream, she believed the verdict and dismissed her desire.

I was that girl, I allowed myself to be discouraged from following my dreams. At that time, I had no encouraging guide nor did I know how to trust in my aspirations. I was naturally shy and disliked competing or being measured against others. Whilst one dream had been shattered, my passion for design and beauty flourished. Although the desire of becoming a performing artist never went away, as it lived itself out at a later time in my life. Working with textiles shaping and creating my own ideas into garments felt rewarding. Being in my own creative space felt satisfying, I loved the solitude, which enabled me to learn at my own pace and I fell in love with every piece I mastered and felt flattered by the admiring words of those who saw me wearing my creations.

Those Who Encourage

The most inspiring people I have crossed paths with, are those who encourage and give support to the fulfilling of our deepest desires. We are all multitalented and have the potential to demonstrate greatness and mastery in all sorts of things. If we do not trust our own abilities we can be easily discouraged by the limited beliefs of others. It is easy to ridicule someone pursuing a dream not yet achieved. Being sensitive or getting offended by unfavourable responses from others does not help. It can crush aspiration instantly, jeopardising all. If we take responsibility for nurturing our dreams, life will furnish us with the strength to move towards them and deliver the opportunities we are searching for.

Throughout my life, I encountered people who tried to tell me that I could only do one thing or another, or that I was not suitable for this or that, or that I couldn't achieve what I dreamed of. I often felt discouraged and was labelled a dreamer and unrealistic. Yet deep down, it felt right to follow my own path as opposed to the one which everyone assumed was right for me. The idea of living a predetermined life mapped out and decided by someone else was never satisfying to me. However, too often I found myself constrained by circumstances, not knowing how to be who I felt I was meant to be.

Everyone has a path, a journey to take. If you feel disheartened by someone's negative opinion about your aspirations, it is because their misguided and limited perspective is projected on to you. Never cease your dreams because of someone's misconception about life.

I frequently questioned the meaning of life. Where had I come from? My place on this planet, and why things happen the way they do. My quest for answers led me to various encounters with philosophers, spiritual guides, and healers. Trying to discover why things were occurring to me in a certain way or figuring out why I existed, was not an easy task. I was confronted with a plethora of answers, some more satisfying than others, but I was disappointed that there was no clear answer. I attained more clarity when I began to experiment with various ideas, exploring and learning to understand the laws that govern our existence.

We are magical and powerful beings, with an ability to manifest our deepest desires, and we are the only ones that can unfold them. Our desires shape us, the moment we let go of our dreams is the moment we lose our identity. I have observed so many who refuse to believe that fulfilling one's desires is possible. I came to discover that aspiration and passion are the magic that makes everything happen, we are all a work in progress. Each day presents new opportunities for innovation, knowledge, and growth that can improve life. Being able to adjust myself was the first step to allow new knowledge, the constant changes I made to my way of thinking and feeling created a platform that enabled me to expand my consciousness and explore to the fullest.

In my late twenties, I chose to explore a monastic form of life, one that is disciplined and controlled. It involved living under vows while studying under the guidance of a spiritual organisation in an attempt to reach some form of spiritual enlightenment. I became a Brahma Kumari (BK) a celibate Yogini sister. Although the seven years I spent as a BK did not lead me to spiritual enlightenment. Instead, it led me to a personal discovery, one which no doctrine, religion, or spiritual leader could possibly reveal. This was my own intuition, the perfect guidance, the key to the fulfilment of my life's purpose.

This was a period in my life when I had given up all my aspirations, believing they would bring me unhappiness. I followed a doctrine that taught denying or inhibiting desires was an honourable act. My dreams were put to bed, and I was overtaken by the wishes of others. I had heard these ideas throughout my life from various sources, my parents, my spiritual leaders, school teachers and even some friends. It dawned on me, during one of the classes I prescriptively attended at the BK's spiritual university, that it could not be the truth. I had reached a point where I could no longer find any logic in this proposition, I could not believe that I had bought into this false premise for so long.

Sitting in front of me was one of the greatest spiritual leaders, one of the ten 'keepers of wisdom' with whom I had studied closely and had also consulted for guidance and advice about my life's affairs. The ideology of a wise, mysterious woman in her nineties, 'Dadi Janki.' I had admired her for her mental strength and her captivating aura, her words seemed profound, and drew me close to her. But this time, as I heard her speak, it felt different. It was as if a veil had been lifted, my own guidance system had somehow kicked in. What this spiritual leader was saying felt wrong and the idea of not allowing my desires felt misguided, even alarming.

I started questioning myself and my previous assumptions. I could see clearly that all of the spiritual leaders I had met were full of desires themselves. While they were encouraging me to deny my dreams to support theirs, they were living and fulfilling their own. I questioned who could possibly determine which aspirations were right or wrong for me and on what basis?

I learned to believe that nothing in life is free, it followed that I was born to earn things. When something did not work out as it should, I felt dejected and questioned my worthiness. I believed that the people or situations around me would be the basis for my happiness.

The reasoning that I must do or become something to be worthy of happiness no longer made any sense. The sense of putting my happiness into someone else's hands did not feel right either. Why should I need to earn or prove my worthiness, and to who, an angry God? Who made up this angry God that looks over us judging our worthiness? How could such an invention be God? This defies everything that God is supposed to represent, in God's eyes, surely, I and everyone on this planet are worthy of the very best from the moment we are born.

Our thoughts and actions define us, aspiration is a powerful force to fuel creation. That is why we feel dissatisfied with a lack of accomplishment when we are not fulfilling our ambitions. Humans are creative. To aspire is part of our beingness. Our capabilities are endless, following our dreams will lead us to do the things we enjoy doing the most. There are many diverse things we can master and still many more we can explore, there are no limits to our learning. Ideas come naturally to most of us but putting them into reality is when real creativity comes to life. A clear mind can quickly turn ideas into reality. We have all experienced those great moments of clarity, those times when our creative juices flow, and we quickly find ways of accomplishing things with ease.

Academically I performed very poorly at school until about age nine, I do not know the exact reason, I was a sensitive and creative child that did not fit the system yet had a great desire to make things better for people. I remember feeling rejected or criticised by my teachers and family. This caused me great anxiety.

My performance changed when I was in my fourth year of school when a new teacher arrived. Miss Kaufman, she was kind and aware of a child's needs. With Miss Kaufman's encouragement and support my anxiety caused by being criticised or punished for not succeeding diminished. I started to enjoy going to school and began to perform well, by the end of the year, my grades had jumped. Maths became one of my favourites, and soon I began to score top marks in most subjects. I remember thinking, 'studying is so easy, why did I not get this before?' Our brain cells perform better when we are happy. Researchers have found that positive children, as an example, put play blocks together much faster and more accurately than children that have been deprived of love, care and encouragement. Being optimistic about the future stimulates feelings of joy and safety, unclouding our minds. Reflecting on my past, I can now understand better why my clarity was often clouded. I allowed myself to be pulled down by many unpleasant external factors.

When we start refocusing towards the things that truly matter such as, ease, love, trust, fun, happiness and satisfaction the quality of our life improves. We all deserve the very best, and there is no reason to deprive ourselves of what makes us feel alive. Knowing how we want to feel is of value, it provides clarity to see where we want to aim in life.

I had to make many mental U turns to orientate towards a better outcome. Obstructions are not always inhibiting they in fact assisted me to identify the right path once I understood how to utilise them. Instead of getting entangled in a hitch whenever something occurred that I did not like. I learned to refocus to my best ability, I started to take responsibility for how I felt. Obstacles became promoters to create new desires and spark new ideas, they became my reminders to focus differently.

When Tragedy Strikes

When I was seventeen, my mother, sister and a family friend died in a car crash. My father and brother survived. The news of the accident shocked me so deeply that I repeatedly fell unconscious. Then the unthinkable happened. Almost exactly one year later, my brother died in another car crash. I adored him and his loss was unbearable. My family was destroyed, and I had to learn to live without them. The loss was almost impossible to comprehend but I knew that I had no choice but to bear the unbearable.

Although I was loved and cared for by my friends and other family members, I felt overwhelmed by the tragedy. Not only was I utterly devastated and ready to give up my life without hesitation if I could make any one of them come back. I also witnessed the pain of loss in everyone's faces around me. Everyone had lost someone, a friend, a wife, a daughter, a son, an aunt or a cousin.

My parents were born into extended Catholic families, on the Italian island of Sicily. My mother was the eldest daughter of seven siblings, and my Father the eldest son, out of five siblings. My grandparents were farmers on this lush volcanic island, they would plant and harvest their own vegetables in the nutritious, richly fertile soil. My grandfather also grew grapes and made his own wine as was the way of life and culture of this beautiful island. My mother was only 22 years old when she gave birth to her first daughter, my eldest sister. My parents were married young and left home to set up life in Germany leaving their first born in the care of my grandparents. Their second daughter, born in Germany, arrived a year and half later. I was the third daughter a year later and then my brother, the youngest born one year after me. My eldest sister joined the family in Germany at three years of age. I was born in the southwest of Germany in a well-kept town called Aalen in the state of Baden-Württemberg.

My parents were programmed to work hard and save money and this is what they did, they had very little time to enjoy their children or to love them the way they would have if they could have been freer. They were too busy working in a confined structure that was set up for labour. However, my parents accumulated a little wealth, purchased their first house in Germany and started building their second home in Sicily. My father took regular trips to Sicily to oversee the construction. I was about 2 years old when my mother received the terrible news that my father had fallen off the scaffolding at the building site and was in a coma. Naturally I was too young to remember but learned about this story later in my life. My father remained in a coma for three days. When he awoke he suffered from severe migraines, unable to work, his mood had become unpredictable with a changeable personality, his pleasant side was overridden by a temperament that was very easily angered. I remember throughout my childhood my parents still in their twenties seeking medical help to cure my father's condition though nothing seemed to help. For small children it was scary growing up in such an environment, home life sometimes could be a turmoil. I grew to resent my father for his harshness and unpredictability, though later I realised that I did not understand the suffering that he was subjected to.

Our family was far from perfect, yet I have fond memories of our holidays spent in Sicily. The wonderful family gatherings, my grandparents, uncles, aunts, cousins and family friends, our holidays were unforgettable adventures with much fun and laughter. There were many of us and so alone time was unheard of. We were never able to go anywhere alone, we would always be accompanied by family members or close family friends. Sometimes as a child I secretly withdrew from the others to spend some time on my own to dream and contemplate and talk to God, to see how I could help to make things better in this world and for my family, I had a grand desire for everyone to reach their highest potential, to make things better and be happy and well.

Whenever the family planned a trip to Sicily, my brother, sisters and I were filled with excitement and eager for the coming holiday. We were fond of Leonforte my parent's village. Arriving there felt like we had been beamed into a different dimension the warm and welcoming culture was so different from what we knew in Germany. In Leonforte things turned magical we had friends and family who jumped with joy to see and be with us. My mother and father's behaviour changed during these long holidays staying with our grandparents. Both felt more loving and carefree particularly my mother, she became so beautiful, surrounded by her large and loving family. To a young couple with four children, it must have felt comforting returning home to such a supportive and beautiful environment.

Sicilian villages are ancient and traditional, the island is surrounded by a shimmering crystal clear sea. The days are enriched with bright blue sunny skies. At night the dark sky is embellished with a myriad of twinkling silver stars. The sun would always shine on our enchanted village even the name Leonforte was part of the fairy tale, it translates into, 'Strong Lion.' Leonforte is nestled inland bordering Mount Etna, which is an active volcano on the east coast of Sicily. From the balcony of our grandparents' house, we had a clear view of Etna. On warm clear summer nights, we would stand on the balcony looking through the railing to marvel at Etna in the distance, spitting red glowing lava that slowly curved and crawled down the volcanic slopes finding its way into the numerous cool streams, to form picturesque rocky gorges that mark some of the most striking spots in Sicily.

The village of Leonforte also graced with the monumental 'Granfonte' that is locally known as the 'Ventiquattru Cannola' the 'twenty four fountains.' Walking distance from my grandparents' house these generous fountains would often turn into our cooling playground on hot summer days. An elongated fountain that stretches twenty four metres in length. A set of ancient steps on either side would lead visitors up to a balcony that projects from the wall of an arched facade holding twenty four bronze spouts, each about one metre apart, gushing fresh spring water into the sunken balcony bassinets. The structure is made up of large sand coloured stone blocks with curved arches that carry ancient engravings, this huge ancient fountain pours ample spring water freely for everyone. The great fountain is a landmark and a meeting place for the local people who during the day come with their water containers to collect their weekly spring water supplies. At night it turned into a romantic spot for local lovers. A truly invigorating sight and a charming novelty for us kids from Germany where the only drinking water we knew came from water bottles or kitchen taps.

Whilst we loved being entertained and refreshed by the gushing waters at the Granfonte, we also ventured to other beauty spots, lush green gardens where orange trees grew, the bright orange fruits hung heavy amongst the leafy branches. I saw an orange tree for the first time in Sicily at about age four. They seemed surreal to my child's eye as I thought oranges came from the supermarket. With our guardians we strolled to other hidden water fountains amongst the sumptuous greenery, where we stopped to collect our drinking water supplies. These springs were considered by the locals as superior fountains. The waters ran over the lava rock of the mountains, picking up as it flowed the minerals and wild herbs that grew beside the streams, gushing straight into our large water containers. It was in Sicily where I learned about the different taste of water and the significance of untampered fresh springs, everyone in Sicily seemed to be a water connoisseur recommending their favoured 'fonte' for the best tasting spring water.

Many Italians had traded this magical place for a life in a more structured modern society, half of my parents' siblings settled in Germany, some of our family members were living in the same neighbourhood, in that sense we had remained a close knit family which also extended to include our Spanish neighbours and their two children. One of those children, Maria, was to become my lifelong friend, Buggi was her nick name.

Nevertheless, we were viewed as outsiders by the German community. As a little girl in the kindergarten and later at school I often endured rejection. I believed my looks were the reason I was not liked. As I looked different, I believed I was not beautiful. I had thick dark curly hair and hazel eyes, I never liked my curly hair and I had far too much of it. The German children had mostly blond hair and blue eyes. So, I regularly prayed to God to make me beautiful as I wanted to be loved. Perhaps my prayers were heard as occasionally people would be dazzled. Strangers would sometimes stop on the street and ask to touch my curly hair calling me adorable, my attractive outlandish features had turned into a novelty. For some Germans I seemed splendid whilst to others I was still labelled an 'Ausländer.' Nevertheless, I grew up becoming a smart young woman who was often complimented for her features.

I always embraced male friendships and felt pretty comfortable around boys, after all I had grown up with my younger brother who had always been my close and best friend, a bond I never kindled with my two sisters. As a teenager I noticed how boys would glance at me with curiosity, although I had not yet developed a particular interest in boys, I could sense genuine desire, but this was not something I wanted to explore. I became curious about the world but had no interest in considering relationships or marriage, besides I was far too young to even contemplate such ideas. But there was one boy who intuitively knew how to sympathetically pursue a friendship and slowly swayed me.

His name was Edgar, nineteen years old, a handsome tall German boy with earnest grey blue eyes. Edgar was athletic, adventurous, charming, intellectual with an above average IQ. I was fourteen when we first became friends as I was still strictly guarded by my parents and had to be home early every evening, a few hours with Edgar were all I was allowed. As we grew closer, I would often sneak out to meet him in secret. To his parent we lied about my age. Our bond became unique, we were each other's first love, and both still innocent. We would scoot off on the back of his motorbike to the prettiest landscaped places where we stopped to stroll along pathways and talked and laughed about everything and nothing.

I never knew that love could feel this exciting, as we were tapping into each other, to discover new things it shaped and moulded me into a new individual. I learned and discovered Edgar was bright and knew so many things. As time passed and I grew a few years older my secret was revealed and I was permitted to have Edgar as my official boyfriend.

I had turned seventeen, my eldest sister had married and moved to Italy with her Italian husband. A family trip was planned to travel from Germany to Italy to visit them at their new home. There was not enough space in the car for everyone so I volunteered to stay home, which of course meant I could spend time with Edgar. I had baked a cheesecake with my mother to be taken as a gift to my sister in Italy but had quarrelled with my mother about the wrapping of the cake. As she was getting ready to depart, I had a feeling of regret. I felt ashamed about my moodiness and decided to apologise. A strong urge came over me to give my mother a big hug as my apology before they drove off. It was a distinctive warm loving hug, we smiled at each other and said goodbye.

This was the first time my family travelled without me, which suited me very well, it felt exciting to have the whole house to myself, this was the first opportunity to spend days and nights with Edgar. Our love had flourished, and we could not bear to be apart for very long. We spent every day and night together, venturing into the surrounding villages on his motorbike. We jogged along country lanes and swam in wild lakes and took long walks into the woodlands with our family dogs, we felt free and the world around us felt mesmerising.

The days passed like the wind and my family were due back. I had received a message earlier in the day from my aunt that they were on their way home. Edgar dropped me home and as I entered the house alone a peculiar sensation came over me, I distinctly felt that nothing would be the same again. My family seemed to be delayed and it was getting late. This was a time before mobile phones and my father had been against installing a telephone in the house, so there was no way to contact them, I could only wait. I fell asleep but with a distinct unease as I was anxious for them to arrive. Not in my wildest imagination was I prepared for what I was about to awaken to. A doorbell ringing relentlessly, it was our next door neighbour Maria our family friend who had received an emergency call and rushed to our home to inform me that the family car had been involved in an accident. It was in the middle of the night, with no phone at home, I made my way through the dark and silent, empty streets to reach the telephone box to call Edgar. I dialled the number and spoke a calmly as possible with my brain swimming in shock. Within a short time, my boyfriend had arrived in his orange Volkswagen Beetle, we drove 30 km to the emergency hospital. It was devastating news the family car had been hit, first by a car, with a sleeping driver. At this point everyone had been shaken but were still okay, then as they exited the damaged car in the darkness and confusion they were hit by a lorry. My brother and father were spared, but my mother who was only forty-two, my sister and her friend who were barely eighteen had been killed.

Nothing can prepare you for something so shocking and tragic, I fainted repeatedly on hearing the news, never having fainted in my life. My brother and I were close, and we comforted each other as best as we could, learning to accept the harsh reality thrust upon us. I shall always remember the trauma on his face it was so hard to accept. My darling brother, he was only sixteen.

Overcome by his inner pain my father fell into a depression first, then later into a victimhood mentality. It was unbearable to live with him, he often lashed out and his anger was uncontrollable. I moved to live with Edgar at his parents' house where we had our own rooms on the top floor. I was welcomed into the family, I had created a bond with his mother Christine. My father retreated to Italy for some time and while he was away, I returned home and stayed with my brother to keep him company in the big empty house.

To seek distraction, I found joy retreating into fashion design and dress making which felt therapeutic. I loved developing my own unique dress style which helped to occupy my mind and keep the thoughts of our irreplaceable loss at bay.

After many months my brother and I slowly started to take part in life's pleasures again. One day we decided to venture out with a group of friends to a smart club in the nearby city of Stuttgart. My brother was to make his own way with his buddies and I was to follow with my friends. As a group of us gathered preparing to leave, getting into our cars, my brother turned around and looked at me, his handsome face beamed and he complimented my tasteful appearance, I sensed he felt proud of his sister.

Later we all met up at the club and talked loudly over the blasting music, and we danced for a while returning to the joy being teenagers.

I felt it was time to leave as it was a longish drive home, and I was the one driving, plus I was glade to escape the noisy club. I turned to my brother to let him know that I would depart to head home with my friend Buggi, we said goodbye and leisurely made our way towards the exit, I intuitively turned around and across the hall I saw my brother standing like a statue rising above the crowd. He looked especially handsome that evening, he was tall with a masculine physique and smartly dressed, as I gazed towards him our eyes briefly met, we cheekily smiled at each other, I noticed a uniquely attractive glowing aura radiating from him.

At home the following morning, the new telephone my father had at last installed was ringing endlessly, it was rather early for a call on Sunday morning. I expected my brother to get up and answer it as he had to be up early since he had been appointed as the ceremonial 'Firmpate' (Life and faith companion) at his friend's 'Firmung' (Confirmation). I ignored the ringing and pulled the cover over to try and sleep some more, yet the ringing endured. Why would my brother not pick up the phone? His room was right next to the living room where the telephone was located. The phone would not stop ringing which seemed strange. Who would call so early on a Sunday morning? These were the thoughts that ran through my sleepy mind.

I eventually gave up and climbed out of bed and in my pyjamas made my way barefoot across the carpeted bedroom floor to our living room and the relentlessly ringing telephone. I glimpsed at the digital clock positioned on the wooden table by the phone, it showed seven am. I placed my hand on the grey receiver to pick up the call and as I did this, the ringing stopped. An indescribable feeling of fear came over me. I knew something terrible had happened. I checked my brother's room, and he was not there. I rushed into the spare bedroom to check on my friend Buggi who had slept over, surprisingly she still slept undisturbed, she had not heard the phone ringing. Feeling desperate I woke her up, 'did you hear the phone?' I asked, 'what phone?' Buggi responded bewildered by my intrusion, she climbed out of bed. I addressed her, 'we have to call the police something has happened,' I rushed back to the phone, Buggi followed, we called the main police station, I gave the route my brother and his friend would have taken to drive home asking if an accident had happened, they confirmed that one had occurred but would not provide details. I became desperate and called the hospital.

By the time the doorbell was rung by the two police officers who had been sent to report to the next of kin, I already had heard the devastating news, my darling brother was gone.

Later I learned of the strange cause of the accident, a blind pedestrian with his guide dog had accidently stepped into the main road, my brother's friend who was driving took action to avoid the man and swung off the road onto the pavement hitting a lamppost, the impact ruptured the petrol tank and the car caught fire, my poor brother was trapped in the front seat unable to escape. Somehow his friend did escape and survived the devastating conflagration

I never found out who called so early that fateful morning, though I asked everyone I could possibly think of. Later I found out that seven am was the exact time of my brother's death. He had been spared the first accident only to succumb to a second one almost to the day a year later. There was much to process through this devastating experience. I felt disoriented, as so much was changing and so very fast, as I was grieving through the loss, I profoundly felt my brother's presence with me, that he had been spared the first time, to be with me through the difficult times, before he could make his exit from this Earth.

Everything around me was falling apart. My five year relationship with Edgar was collapsing. Overcome by the stress of my loss and pain our carefree connection was challenged. I felt the need to retreat, to be alone, solo, and unrestricted as there was nothing I could give in my grief. I felt broken, all who I had loved were gone, I had been thrown out of balance and was struggling to deal with loss upon loss. My almost perfect five years relationship with Edgar took a U-turn and ended in tragedy. Somehow a part of me wanted it to end, I was on a vibrational downward spiral. I secretly wished that Edgar would find someone else to be with so I would not need to break his heart, as I did not have the courage to break up with him nor did I know what reason I should give. However, I never would have imagined that Edgar who I trusted so much would do what he did.

He secretly kindled an affair with a close friend, so it was my heart that got broken instead. I felt deceived by my first love in the midst of my grief, the man I once admired had turned into a coward and had betrayed me with a girl who had posed as my best friend for months but turned out to be a cheat. My heart had never been broken before. I did not know the abject pain that would follow such a deception. For all I knew both were suited for each other with an affair kindled on falsehood. When Edgar tried to make a comeback. I knew what I truly desired was to be free from both.

'Take care of what you wish for.'

Looking back, I can see clearly although it had turned out distorted, I had not wished for a deception of this kind. That what I had wished for had realised. Since I had a solid momentum of loss and pain, my wish manifested itself, to match my current vibration.

Help on the Way

I could not bear the pain or the thought that people would look on me with pity. In search of release from all the grief, I took the first available opportunity to escape the environment that bound me to those memories. I moved away from home with my close family friend Buggi, we had grown up together and she had been my deceased sister's best friend. We decided to move to Ulm for a while and then to Munich to attend further studies far away from home, where no one would know about my tragedies.

Embracing a new city life distracted me from my grief. I wanted to forget all that had happened and speak to no one about it. I was desperately seeking relief and longed for freedom from the constant pain of loss. I had millions of questions about the meaning of life and wanted explanations. I was debating in my mind the rights and wrongs of life but was left confused and estranged. When happiness is absent for a long time, it can feel like happiness is a misapprehension, and feeling bad becomes the norm. It seemed there was no escape from the grief that was lingering within me.

After the death of most of my family I felt like I was the unhappiest girl in the world. I gained weight. I had been a healthy, slim teenager weighing 45 kg with a height of 1.68m. Two years later, I found myself weighing 58 kg. I could not understand how this had happened and I did not like my body or myself very much. At that time, I had no idea how to change my situation. Years later I learned that unhappiness can cause weight gain. The anxiety I was feeling caused my body to produce Cortisol that resulted in weight gain. Cortisol is a hormone that our body produces when we are stressed. This can stimulate cravings for sweet, high fat, and salty foods. I had also developed verrucae on one of my feet which seemed untreatable. I was seen by specialist doctors for over two years who did their best to prescribe me cures, they also made repeated attempts to cut them out and yet they just came back and got worse, eventually covering half of my foot. The cause was diagnosed as emotional stress. Yet no doctor I visited, guided or informed me how to become free of stress.

Barely nineteen, abandoned and broken with deception, loss and grief. All this unhappiness I was locked into, triggered a desire to be free. What I truly wanted was to feel good about myself. I knew that I had some serious cleaning up to do, I did not know how yet, but I knew I had to change. All I could do was to reach within myself for the love that was buried somewhere inside of me, which is the only aspect of me that I could at this point focus on. So, myself reliance and spiritual growth began to rise, the expansion of my unity consciousness was launched.

Detox

'When our life moves towards one extreme, we have the potential to draw it to the opposite extreme, the greater the suffering, the greater the potential for happiness.'

Happiness is a vital ingredient for wellbeing. At the age of nineteen, I decided to undergo a juice detox for six weeks, inspired by a book I had read. This book was authored by Dr Otto Buchinger, a German physician, an admirable philosopher, and a pioneer of therapeutic fasting. I followed the guidance laid out in his book. Although my initial plan was only to juice fast for seven days, I kept juicing for six weeks, this juice fast completely changed my perspective of life. In my first week of detoxing, I experienced mood swings so intense that I began to feel aggravated by everyone around me. My body temperature dropped, and I sat in our living room wrapped in a blanket feeling cold with the heating on at full blast, with my friend Buggi sitting next to me, shaking her head and sweating in her cotton tank top, patiently bearing it all. I kept juicing and did daily colonic cleansing as instructed in the book. I also took natural vitamin supplements to ensure my body received all the nutrients it needed.

In addition to juice, I also consumed over two litres of water every day. Our body is mostly water, and benefits from drinking plenty. Water acts as a carrier increasing the transmission of energy around the body, and therefore our wellbeing. Our bladder's capacity naturally grows as we consume more water. My detox took me deep and threw the unexpected at me. Juice fasting is as much a physical detox as it is an emotional detox. What I felt happening whilst cleansing was the surfacing of old locked in emotional patterns, ready to be cleansed. It is a releasing process which comes up to be felt, faced and released. It is most common, to have emotional fits during fasting, this is the time when you experience all that needs to go. Magic happened as emotional energies and physical toxins made their way out of my body. As a result, my body felt less tense, lighter and freer. With all the ups and downs during my juice fast came a shift in consciousness.

As I reached day four of my juice fast, I felt my energy shifting and I slowly began to feel stronger. My body called for movement, I had an extreme desire to exercise, and I found myself performing sports four to five hours a day. The verrucae on my foot cleared like magic completely vanishing within ten days and have never returned. I had not imagined anything like this would be possible. I felt like a superwoman thriving solely on liquids, my skin was glowing, and life started to look rosy again.

I had such a remarkable result, mentally and physically from my first juice detox that this form of cleansing became part of my life. My first juice detox was six weeks long, I often think back amazed at myself, how I sustained six weeks so easily. There is much more to juice fasting than just drinking juice.

My six week detox became a building block for me to move forward with my life in a very different way. My fasting experience had taught me how to listen to my senses, my cells telling me precisely whether food or drink is right, by how I feel when it is digested. Our body is nourished by the quality of energy that is stored in the food and drink we eat. Yet food and drink are not the only sources that nourish our bodies.

I had many glimpses of being nourished and rejuvenated by a form of energy, during juice fasting, which I understand today to be a high frequency energy. I cannot explain this phenomenon, but I felt it happening. I felt high during fasting. I noticed as I was breathing deeply that the pure air nourished me, I felt my mind was freeing up.

In the early times of my juice fasting experiences, I did not know about Breatharians, who obtain all their nutrients through the elements, air or sunlight without the need for food and water. I had no idea this was even possible.

I later learned about a lifeforce known as Prana, Chi, or Manas or in Western countries known as Life Energy or Universal energy. I researched this phenomenon and found reports of humans that live on this energy without the need of consuming food. Who are referred to as Breatharian. Some Breatharians eat a little, perhaps a piece of fruit not more than three times a week.

You may think it is not possible to live on air or sunlight alone. However, consider that our plant life thrives by drawing nutrients from the elements around them and many wild animals thrive consuming very little food, particular during hibernation.

Cleansing the inside of my body regularly remains vital. Now living in London, a big busy city with plenty of pollution and toxic energy. I still juice fast regularly, one of the most incredible things about the juice detox is that when I resume eating solid food it feels new and immensely satisfying, as if I was tasting food for the first time.

Juice fasting soothed my emotional pain and opened a completely new understanding of life and death connecting me deeply to a non-physical aspect of me. The Dr Buchinger juice fast clinic in Marbella Spain was one of the first juice fast retreats I visited which by then was run by Dr Buchinger's daughter. My preferred holidays have been exploring various juice fasting retreats around the world, each having its bespoke traditions. I visited a unique family run juice fast sanctuary in Italy also I visited juice fast retreats in Thailand and Turkey finding that they all had their individual approach. I learnt so much from those great experiences and based upon the knowledge I acquired I improved and advanced my own juice fasting technique.

Our bodies decline because of various causes, loss, fear, stress, worry and unhappiness are triggers. We feel those emotions and when we do, we know that our health is being compromised. If uncared for those emotions will manifest as illnesses. Ageing of course, is also a cause of decline. This can be halted by healing which can be substantially helped when we support our cells by supplying the right nourishment. Every cell in our body listens to our thoughts. When our thoughts are cleansed, our cells are too, healthy thoughts are powerful.

Fasting is not suffering or deprivation, it is for cleansing and fine tuning your higher frequencies. As a result of the cleanse, you can tune into a higher frequency space. The body is composed of trillions of intelligent cells, each cell can restore and develop itself.

Our body cells replace themselves every seven to ten years. This means that our organs, such as our skin, liver and heart become renewed as old cells die and are replaced by new ones. The cell renewal process takes place in our bodies from head to toe. Some organs rejuvenate slower than others such as bone which can take longer. Rejuvenation causes our skin to flake off constantly, evidenced by the dust in our homes which partly consists of dead skin cells. The most visible examples of renewal are our perpetually growing nails and our hair which constantly falls out and regrows. Learning this you may wonder just like I did. If our bodies are rejuvenated with brand new cells, why do our bodies age?

So, I researched deeper and found that ageing lies not simply in our cells but in the atoms which are the components that the body's cells consist of and those are replaced each year. Most new atoms are taken in through the air we breathe and the food and liquids we consume. The body renews itself at a varying pace.

How long each cell in certain areas last depends on how much work they are asked to do. Whilst we may not be able to stop the body's ageing process completely, we can slow it down and assist the cells in the rejuvenation process. This we can do by helping our cells to detox. Our cells will do the rest.

High Frequency Nourishment

My regular fasting and cleansing have slowed down my ageing process and kept my body young and flexible. My appearance is often mistaken for a woman 15-20 years my junior. I have also experienced how clean cells raise frequency easily and intuitively, aligning to a higher frequency. One can comprehend it in this way. My cells are drawing in 'chi' a divine life force which are photon light nutrients emitted by the Sun that nourish the body. This is how Breatharians maintain a balanced body weight effortlessly. Experiences like this happen during fasting as my body cells rejuvenate and my wellbeing rises to a higher vibrational sensation, I can draw in those frequencies moment by moment depending on my alignment capability. It is a bit like falling in love we get all blissed out, happily roaming around with no desire to eat. Do you remember this sensation?

Now you see fasting is not about depriving yourself, and not meant to be a struggle but a wondrous and uplifting experience. A cleansing process allowing the aligning of the body to additionally nourish itself through other means than eating.

Our body's cells draw in energy from food that we eat but if our diet includes animal products, the tortured energy of an animal's suffering gets impregnated into their flesh. Animals release all sorts of fear and stress hormones during their abuse. This is not good as it is dense, negative energy.

The detoxing process is the letting go of those low frequency energies that have settled in our bodies, causing harm to our cells or blocking our natural 'chi flow'. To align with higher frequencies, we need to release and cleanse low frequency toxins we have consumed and turn our joy level up a notch. Our body's cells will rejuvenate and align to receive the nourishment of high frequency light photons. Naturally if the body is full of the dense energy and heavy toxins present in meat and processed food one will struggle to fast, and it will feel forced.

This is the moment to ask oneself. What energy am I holding in my body cells? What am I eating? Am I eating suffering and emotional torture? Ask yourself! I hear people saying things like, 'I could never fast,' or 'I feel ill if I don't eat.' Well those people are often ill due to what they eat and breath. If we do not set up the right environment it will feel like a struggle and deprivation to fast. First prepare properly for the fast depending on the toxic level the body holds both mentally and physically and then it will become a pleasing and freeing experience. If one attempts to fast from a dense low frequency state it will be difficult to accomplish a long fast and will not make it past the first two days before feeling overcome by the craving for food. Those that are big on meat consumption or animal product in general will need to transmute those dense energies first. To prepare for a fast, practise meditation by aligning with high frequency this will mentally and intuitively guide a transition to vegan food. Allow the body to adjust, introduce healthy smoothies and juices, and fresh raw vegetables, into daily meals. Inspire yourself to exercise and spend time in nature. This will easily allow a transition to a fasting cleanse without struggle.

With good nutrition our skin will glow and can even create an ability to give some protection from Sun exposure. I noticed this during a juice fast, I was literally drinking my sunscreen. The juice from green plants was helping my skin to respond to the Sun more efficiently. The Sun emits a potent life energy in the form of photon light particles. Plants convert this light energy into usable energy and so can the cells in our bodies. Vegetables that absorb a lot of Sunlight are the healthiest and most nutritious foods to consume. Plants use photosynthesis which is the transformation of energy from Sunlight into plant growth which in turn produces consumable fuel. The Sunlight that is absorbed by these organisms is stored in the form of biophotons which are components of light energy, this is what makes raw fruit and vegetables one of the best sources of natural energy. Fruit and vegetables are living when harvested, staying this way until eaten raw cooked or made into juice. This means that juice fasting is an extremely powerful way of healing and restoring the body's cells. Our DNA reads frequency constantly.

Our nervous system is an operational aerial, and the Earth has a reservoir of energy that is created by the power of the Sun. We are electrical light beings with a body that is nourished by the light energy provided by the Sun. The healthier and cleaner our cells become the easier it is to draw in the chi life force, it will happen instinctively. My best fasting experience is when I am within nature away from the dense energies that constantly need transmuting in a city like London where I live. Throughout a juice fast my body undergoes the deep clean in stages. In the first three to four days, it expels the accessible toxins lingering in my body. Sometimes by expelling toxins through sweating at night, my tongue gets coated even after cleaning, by the time I reach day eight when the first cycle is completed the coating on my tongue clears. As my fast continues the next deeper cleansing cycle begins reaching around the tenth day. The tongue gets coated again but it clears faster, many emotions, sensations and memories rise to the surface, stuff I had long forgotten waiting to be cleansed. In between all of this I often get highs of wellbeing. I feel excited about life, this is when the desire to take juices for nourishment reduces. Food becomes irrelevant and uninteresting as my spiritual experience spirals. The desire to be in nature and bond with nature increases, at this point my body intuitively starts drawing light photons automatically. There is no struggle and no feeling of deprivation, I feel nourished, satisfied and blissful. My juice intake becomes minimal at one or two glasses per day.

I always drink my juices raw and cold pressed, some of the most effective hydrating juices I enjoy drinking alone are as follows: Celery, carrot, tomato, apple, watermelon, honeydew melon, cucumber, grapefruit, coconut water, aloe vera juice, cranberry, grape and lime or lemon. I also love adding lots of ginger to all of them and mint to some. They also taste delicious mixed together. Below are three of my favourite juice combinations:

- Celery, lemon, and ginger.
- Celery, lemon, apple, tomato and ginger.
- Cucumber, honeydew melon, lemon, and ginger.

Water is another natural miracle, we use it every day, our bodies are predominantly water. I unquestionably have experienced the uplifting and healing powers water holds. I see water as something magical, its therapeutic nature feels soothing and healing, either from drinking or immersion, pure natural water enriches life. I am a keen swimmer, I learned how to swim at the age of three. I love water. It is critical to my wellbeing and happiness.

It is important to note that not all water is the same. To ensure we are utilising the right kind of water we should obtain it from a pure spring, or we can program it. Water is programmable just like crystals. Cymatics is a science that explains how sound influences the structure of water. It has been found that water can hold a 'memory' transmuted through the sound of human intentions. The works of Masaru Emoto may be studied which explain these fascinating findings in more detail. Demonstrating how when we clearly visualise an intention, such as gratitude towards the water it takes shape in the form of a single structure like a snowflake. What this means is that we can intentionally program the water we drink, cook with, or use to wash and bathe, with words and thoughts. This is also applicable to our body which is mostly water. We can therefore instruct our bodies which is a fascinating way to control how we wish to feel. I use this practice before drinking. I speak to my water saying words like, health, vitality, nutrition, love, happiness. I do the same when I am in a steam room circulating happy intentions by programming the water drops that the pores of my skin absorb.

Earth has an abundance of resources we can draw from to maintain our physical and emotional health. Through grounding or earthing we can draw the right kind of free electrons that provide our bodies with amazing health benefits. When we walk barefoot or let our skin touch the earth, we exchange electrons. This ground or earths us, electrically reconnecting us to the Earth. Those electrons we draw into our bodies from the Earth neutralise any damaged frequencies. This is a wonderful way of keeping healthy. I love walking barefoot on grass or sandy beaches or sitting on rocks and placing my hands on them. Swimming in the sea or in mineral rich water, also grounds you, this is wellbeing flowing through the body.

Our planet Gaia is a living being just like us and loves us so much, making conscious contact through grounding triggers us into a blissful state. One can also use grounding to heal pain in the body, find a clean, safe, and high frequency spot to sleep directly on the ground, preferably grassy ground or on a large rock or within proximity to it. One can practise this as an afternoon nap. While sleeping on the ground we can upload healing energy from the Earth's magnetic field. This transmission of data restores our cells. Remember, we can benefit from the Earth by walking bare foot on healthy terrain.

Our Stomach the Second Brain

What we feed ourselves is important, I understand myself to be multidimensional, a soul aspect of me known as Ivana experiencing life on this planet. I am composed of the eternal form, a part of my higher consciousness, which is seated in the centre of my forehead, near my brain. Which is also referred to as the third eye. This soul aspect gives life to my body and makes my body spark and function in many ways. I see my body's senses as the mechanism that allows me to express myself and experience this world.

Appreciating my body and looking after my health and appearance is a positive way of living. There are plenty of people that may see it as vanity and something to be condemned. But from my own experience, this has always served me well. An enjoyable and positive way of thinking and feeling, facilitates a healthy lifestyle.

Our body is an organism that wants to move. I exercise regularly, I run, walk, swim, skate, dance, stretch and cycle. I love the way my body feels when I stretch and breathe in deeply. When I am not juice fasting, I fuel my body with predominantly raw and fresh plant based food mostly organic. My water at home is fluoride free I produce my own distilled water for drinking and cooking with. What you feed your body the most will become what your body's cells crave so you may as well make it crave healthy food. My interest in healthy foods started when I was a teenager, and I have been a vegetarian turned vegan for most of my life. It is truly worth ensuring that the body functions at its best, I have made this one of my top priorities, which became even clearer during my unhealthy spinoffs.

I have always been passionate about healthy living. I did not drink alcohol until my mid-twenties, when my curiosity led me to experiment with drinking as well as smoking and sniffing cocaine on nights out in London. Whilst using those stimulants I realised that I had lost control of my own faculties and behaviour, making me undeniably unattractive, there was no long term satisfaction with those experiments and this trial was short lived. After several stints of humiliation, I decided that my natural high seemed far more exciting and sustainable. I stopped taking the drug, dismissed smoking and drinking, and focused on how to get high on living life rather than destroying it.

I found alcohol to be one of the fastest liquids to lower vibration. It also damages the skin, enlarging the pores and making it reddish and unhealthy looking. Those that drink alcohol will for sure have experienced the unpleasant after effect caused by it. The tangible evidence often followed by downheartedness, mood swings or even worse, depression. The consumption of alcohol is too well promoted in our society and is a primary tool used to keep humanity at a low state of consciousness. It has been used as such for thousands of years. The word alcohol is known to have derived from the Arabic words Al Kuhl and Al Gawl which mean body eating spirit. Perhaps this is why alcoholic drinks are called spirits? These words which sound like alcohol are most likely where the English word 'ghoul' is derived from.

The Pineal Gland

The Pineal gland is a unique organ. A healthy functional Pineal gland is vital for optimal health. Bioelectrochemistry and Bioenergetics analysts found that the Pineal's tissues contained noncentrosymmetric crystals, proving the presence of Piezoelectricity. Piezoelectricity is the electric charge also found in crystals. Crystals are often used as a transmitter and amplifier in technology. They further observed calcifications on the Pineal tissues like that of hydroxyapatite, plus aluminium.

This gland has the highest calcification rate among all organs in the body. The Pineal gland's activation is key to expanding consciousness, inner vision, and wisdom, it is often referred to as the third eye. It is in the centre of the brain, above and behind the pituitary gland. Its function is to supply the body with melatonin, an anti-aging and anti-stress hormone that affects our mood, immune system, and sleep. When the release of melatonin is disrupted, mood swings and depression can be experienced, the activation of the Pineal gland also processes neurochemicals such as Pinoline and DMT.

DMT is also referred to as the Spirit Molecules, that connect the mind and body. DMT is produced in the Pineal gland during deep meditation, sexual ecstasy, extreme physical stress, and near death experiences. A healthy activated Pineal gland, provides deep spiritual experience, melatonin quietens the body and mind, the gland acts like a transmitter or amplifier, allowing access to higher consciousness. Pinoline and DMT, are psychoactive, causing changes in perception, mood, awareness, and behaviour. The Pineal gland decalcification can be done by focusing on beauty and love, laughing, or smiling, toning with sounds such as chanting, tapping, breathing deeply, spending time with nature and animals, eating healthy, nutritious, organic, vegan raw food.

Vaccination, fluoride, toxic medicine, polluted air, stress, fear, unhealthy low vibrational food, alcohol, smoking, caffeine, sugar, artificial food ingredients hormones, and additives that are in processed foods, dim the activation of the Pineal gland thus dimming spiritual development, that aligns us to our superpowers.

Weather Manipulation Crazy Stuff!

Is someone spraying our skies at night whilst we are asleep? Aluminium oxide, iodide, barium, potassium, strontium, copper sulphate is some of the ingredients. Sweet dreams!

The United Kingdom had gone into lockdown, it was the 16th of March 2020, the people of London had shut themselves in their homes. Stores, shops, pubs and restaurants were ordered to close. The first day of a nationwide lockdown, no aircraft in the sky and no traffic in the streets, the roads of London were empty and continued to be empty for weeks. No air traffic, no cars, no trucks, the streets devoid of vehicles, a truly historic moment. The government in conjunction with the mass media by announcing a deadly pandemic contrived to convince the country that there was a deadly virus called Covid 19 lingering at everyone's doorstep and hanging in the air waiting to strike. As usual I ignored the media fiction, not for one second did I believe the news of a pandemic. Whilst most of London was subservient and under lockdown I continued with my daily lifestyle and took pleasure in cycling through the empty and tranquil streets of London.

As I was cheerfully peddling on my white town bike through the abandoned London streets, I noticed something different and special, about the air I was breathing. Never has London air felt so clean, each breath I took tasted delicious. This strange unprecedented government order had brought about something positive. Within only a couple of days following the March 2020 lockdown, the climate in London had transformed and presented the most favourable weather patterns.

A massive improvement in air quality with increased sunlight, the skies were crystal clear and had turned a vibrant blue, creating an atmosphere I had never witnessed in the metropolis before. The plants and flowers in the public parks and residential gardens shot up and were sprouting leaves and blooms plentifully in lush vibrant colours, my neighbourhood looked vividly bright and fresh as never before. London's climate had changed radically. The lockdown had inadvertently created the most magnificent spring, the month of May was the sunniest month on record for all of England. Many people shared social media posts when they saw the same thing happening across Europe, clean fresh air and the hitherto polluted lakes, rivers and streams entered into a self-cleaning phenomenon returning water to its original quality and purity. The strangest thing was that this radical environmental improvement was hardly mentioned by the mass media who were fixated hysterically on the Covid 19 pandemic.

London's usual weather entails moody rain fall. though the rain is frequent it is not as heavy as the impression many have of London. We nearly always have overcast sky in the Winter and Autumn with intermittent Sunshine in the Spring and perhaps a little more in the Summer. The pollution is high in London and as a result I often get itchy eyes. I can feel scratchy particles entering my eyes when I walk or cycle through the city, I also have a constant runny nose when out in London no matter the season. All of these allergic reactions rapidly disappeared during the first lockdown as the air pollution cleared away.

Before the 2020 March lockdown I had observed aircraft crossing over London and wondered about the vast amounts of contrails. Why would some aircraft have short contrails that would evaporate almost immediately? But some aircraft would leave contrails very long and dense, although these aircraft would be appearing in the sky at a similar time and in similar conditions. We all see the jet aircraft created contrails in our skies, some are short and evaporate immediately then others are thick copious long trails often appearing as criss-crosses lingering in the sky long after the aeroplane has passed. I noticed a strange recurring coincidence that whenever we had blue skies in London, thick long contrails appear in the sky, and not long after that, the blue skies change into a dirty grey carpet of thick cloud as opposed to natural white fluffy clouds. I have been gazing at the sky all of my life, and I certainly do not remember it looking like this in the eighties when I was growing up.

Those dense trails I believe to be chemicals sprayed to modify the weather and pollute our environment. They are known as 'The chemtrail spraying operation.' The reason for this and who is responsible I have no full explanation as yet, though what I have learned is that, weather modification or control, is the deliberate altering of the weather. It has been conducted throughout the latter part of the 20th century.

'Cloud seeding' is commonly used to urge rainfall or create snowfall for local water supplies. It has also been used in warfare as a military strategy to direct destructive weather conditions towards the enemy. The CIA sponsored Operation Popeye which was a chemical weather modification programme during the Vietnam war between 1967 to 1972, is a historical example of where clouds were maliciously seeded by the USAF to prolong the monsoon over the route of the Ho Chi Minh Trail which was used to move military supplies from North Vietnam through Laos and Cambodia into South Vietnam. Solar geoengineering is a further technique known as Earth cooling strategies, this adds particles to the sky or manipulates clouds in the atmosphere to reduce the amount of sunlight that reaches the Earth's surface. Weather modification, along with climate engineering are well documented yet argued against as conspiracy theories. It has been banned by the United Nations under the Environmental Modification Convention. Despite this China has launched the world's largest weather control mechanism that has a capacity to produce up to 10 billion cubic metres of rainfall each year. This system can modify weather across an area the size of Alaska. Saudi Arabia has also been cloud seeding since 2000 with an aim to increase rainfall over its dry parched desert landscape. Some of the chemical materials used are potassium chloride, sodium chloride and magnesium plus others.

Authorities deny the existence of chemtrails stating that chemtrails are nothing more than ice crystals. Perhaps that dismissive explanation may be feasible in the winter, but does not seem logical on hot summer days at a height of seven miles, ice crystals would surely be heavy enough to succumb to gravity and drop to earth or evaporate instantly. Authorities can give all sorts of 'weather expert' explanations as to why we have heavy trails lingering in our skies. But one can also research factual reports of countless independent investigations that confirm findings of poisonous chemicals and materials that are being dispersed into our environment; some are yellow fungal mould spores, barium and cadmium, plus, radioactive thorium, the most sprayed material is aluminium. These are materials and chemicals that are known to harm our central nervous system causing emotional instability, disturbed sleep, memory loss, nervousness, headaches, and many other ailments. Perhaps this explains why so many people's emotional state is in flux. One must consider the sheer quantity of prescription drugs that are distributed and consumed for these sorts of ailments and the industry built around suppling them.

Health Masters and Magicians

If our authorities feel it necessary to constantly coerce, remind, censor information, disincentivise, bully, socially shame, guilt trip, threaten, punish, or criminalise the population to gain compliance, we can be certain what they are promoting is not for the benefit of our health. I observed the falsehoods disseminated by the news channels and by our government. I felt misled. Also, the pharmaceutical industries that promoted highly toxic vaccines, selling medical products that would create dependency, whilst concealing alternative healing methods. I also noticed the manipulation within the food industry, the financial system, religion, political structures, and the Hollywood entertainment industry. Literally every subject the main media covers. Our media groups have deceived people about their wellbeing since its existence, skilfully promoting products that are detrimental to human health and our environment.

Social media companies are set up to censor and debunk posted facts that go against the tales of the big headlines. I question. How is it that the social media companies cannot eliminate online child grooming and child pornography? but have the technology to censor so called conspiracy theories which challenge and offer alternative views to the untruths pedalled through these channels.

'The level the world has been deceived is inconceivable. But how are they able to do this? Because we let them do it!'

We have been frightened by the authorities to surrender our capability of judgement, and have allowed them to trap us in our homes, while obedient entities have been given authority to discriminate, and ridiculed those that question the narrative of our media. News reports are no more than staged and scripted acts performed by alliances of those who wish to enslave humanity. We have all been deceived, and the reason this puppet show keeps going day after day is because of the population's collective belief in what is broadcast and disseminated.

Real leaders do not need to exploit. True leaders will empower not mute and demoralise their people, true leaders will guide people with wisdom to discover their own given abilities that lead to self-empowerment. Imagine how beautiful this planet would be if wellbeing would be marketed by our media instead of fear.

Figuring out my own way, instead of following the masses, made me undeniably the odd one out, but how could I possibly trust a system that misleads people about their health over exploits the resources of our planet, consents to the brutality of animal slaughter, uses the beautiful animals of our world to supply fur and leather goods and sells their unhealthy flesh and blood for human consumption as if it be the most normal thing in the world to do.

I felt perplexed by how certain people labelled me as too extreme for being vegan. People who believe that someone who stands apart from the masses refusing to contribute to the slaughter and cruelty that is committed against our beautiful animal kingdom is extreme? Whilst those same people eat the flesh of animal corpses for dinner and think it is normal? The hypocrisy is plain to see.

'Following the truth was far more important to me than being liked.'

People have been brainwashed to such an extreme that they accept violence as the norm and caring love as extremism. How many have been duped into believing the righteousness of wars? What insanity has been sold to the people? We have a government that divides us, nature versus technology, humanity versus animals, racism versus unity, rich versus poor, old versus young, this is the trap that keeps us prisoners.

Our society does not understand the energy of the violence that is spread by animal consumption. Eating animal products is an addiction, many feel it is wrong, yet cannot stop eating it. Should we ask why the flesh and dairy products that people consume have this kind of addictive effect? Consider the stress factor of not only the animals that are being slaughtered but also the people that work in the slaughterhouses and the food industries. Imagine what this does to their conscience.

The meat of cattle, pigs, lambs, and chickens that are bred in the most horrific conditions is unhealthy. The chickens are kept in small metal boxes on top of one another, they cannot see daylight, farm animals are fed steroids and antibiotics. They are not raised with care or love, ask yourself; where do all those steroids, drugs and released negative violent energy end up? On your dinner table and you are consuming and absorbing them.

"The greatness of a nation and its moral progress can be judged by the way its animals are treated." Mahatma Gandhi.

Any authority capable of setting up such crimes is not far off having those acts transferred to humans. If one digs deeper into the unspeakable, maybe one day you will wake up and learn that Hollywood's paedophilia ring may very well be true and that the world is being ruled by a small group of malevolent beings that perform rituals at key vortex points around the world so that the terror and horror that enters the Earth's energetic grid, affects the Earth's magnetic field. Many slaughterhouses around the world are built on such energy vortexes, to hold down vibrational frequency, lowering human consciousness, in an attempt to prevent the human race discovering how powerful and what magnificent creators they truly are.

One may say, 'well what can we do?' our freedom has been taken, and we are surrounded by those influences. Well, I say we still have our freedom to think independently, and we have a choice to listen to our emotions. We can go outdoors with nature, breath in deeply, connect with the elements, our planet, our animal kingdom, and our fellow humans while looking deeply into their eyes, feel them and the connection we naturally have for one another. We also have the option to turn off the televisions and detox from the media and say no to injustice.

Once there is willingness to change, the body tells us what it wants as it attempts to raise its vibration to build a healthier physicality at a higher frequency, then it will not tolerate low vibrational foods.

Is Contagion a Myth?

I have witnessed much controversy in our healthcare system, which I view as a controlled scheme. I truly do not need a doctor or anyone else to tell me whether I am healthy, I can figure this out for myself based on how I feel. The body is an intelligent organism it tells you when something is not working, it is that simple. We can all tune into our bodies and learn how to become our own doctor. A majority of doctors whether knowingly or not, are trained to serve the big pharmaceutical companies and not humanity. Usually, they know very little about health and nutrition. They have memorised a given script that teaches a unified policy for the distribution of pharmaceuticals to keep people dependant on drugs.

Natural and herbal medicine was widely accepted in America up to 1900. Almost half the doctors and medical colleges in the United States practised holistic medicine, utilising data from Europe and from native Americans. Those practices were stopped by a man named Abraham Flexner who travelled around the country to report on the status of medical education and concluded that all the natural healing modalities which had been practised for hundreds of years were, 'unscientific quackery.' Although Flexner neither trained nor practised as a physician. Flexner was appointed by the Rockefeller Foundation to reform medical education. Thus, beginning the trend for modern medicines made from petrochemicals produced by pharmaceutical companies that can be patented, monopolised, and sold for high profits. The average junior doctor or medical trainee is fed theoretical papers that have been reviewed and approved by a general education board, to be memorised to obtain a master's degree or PHD. Education boards are funded by those that wish to control the medical institutions and the education of medical practitioners for political and financial gain. Whilst many of those medical scholars have studied for years, when they are taken into nature to observe and listen to wondrous yet unexplainable things, most will not believe what does not match their academic studies. How can everyone thinking the same way be good for scientific research? There are new advances being made by some scientists that go against the system, but these advances are never given equal status to the controlled mainstream and therefore these scientific discoveries are held back.

My plan for a healthy lifestyle has served me well. It kept me healthy, flexible, fit and out of the GP's surgery. I considered this success was reason enough to explore further. I started as a teenager to mistrust the common medical advice provided by the average doctor as it often made no sense. From the unhealthy food that hospitals served to patients, to the calculated encouragement of patient's dependency on medication. This did not look healthy to me. I had a natural interest in healthy living and explored plenty of alternative methods that kept me, and others healthy, most average doctors had no clue about them. I was rather surprised to learn that many doctors were smokers and lived unhealthy lifestyles, which made no sense as I had envisaged that doctors would represent good health practice in their personal lifestyle, which in turn would be passed on to their patients.

What truly are most of our doctors and medical practitioners today? The typical doctor is little more than a drug dealer, prescribing medication on behalf of the massive pharmaceutical industry that dominates medical providers with huge marketing campaigns to prescribe and recommend specific brands. Because of this few people educate themselves about true health, resulting in their not knowing how to take care of their bodies. Our bodies respond and thrive with love and high vibrational food.

When the COVID 19 pandemic was announced in London March 2020 I could not accept it as a truth, as I considered the claimed contagiousness to be a myth. I understood frequency and health and had no reason to doubt my learning. Since my findings and my own experiences led me to view things differently, I follow alternative and innovative medical science that researches our body's healing power. When our body is worn or stressed our cells are challenged.

Dr Thomas Cowan MD carried out research which points to how our body produces a virus to heal but is not is passed on. Therefore, it is a virus that is not contagious but something our body produces when cells in our body create exosomes to remove dead cells and toxins to heal. Exosomes cannot be passed on, the body produces them to start the healing process. Equally, if one feels distressed it attracts people that feel the same, a person's body can detox at the same or similar time as others around them which gives the illusion of contagion. In his book 'Contagion is a Myth,' Dr Thomas references chemist Louis Pasteur 1822–1895 who convinced the medical community that contagious germs cause disease 'Pasteur germ theory' was then adopted as the approved reason for illness. Dr Thomas further references Pasteur's private diaries, where the chemist admitted that his entire effort to evidence contagion was a failure, confessing on his deathbed that, 'the germ is nothing, the terrain is everything.'

It is agonising listening to the nonsensical 'experts' that appear on mainstream media pushing hard to sell a toxic drug labelled as a vaccine to prevent COVID 19, none of these vaccines have completed thorough research trials, and all companies producing the vaccines appear to be free of liability even if it harms or kills the recipient. Whilst natural remedies are ignored, censored, or ridiculed, a nonstop overwhelming marketing campaign has been run to brainwash people to believe that this vaccine is the only way to combat the COVID 19 virus, they label this experimental drug a scientific breakthrough, when in fact it is against all good scientific practice.

Our bodies are magnificent mechanisms which have strong immune systems capable of self-healing. To inject oneself with unknown components which are foreign to the body, jeopardises the function of this healthy natural immune system and will potentially lead to illness or death. It is necessary to be self-educated and use our intuition and logic when it comes to our health. We are constantly fed misleading stories regarding healthcare. Breathing in fresh air freely and not restricting our respiratory function is vital for optimum health. Constantly wearing a mask can lead to encephalopathy causing brain damage. Bacterial growth encouraged by mask wearing was a leading cause of death in the Spanish Flu epidemic 1918/1920.

Radiologist Dr Gerd Reuther, is a German author who has recorded his research in the widely acclaimed bestseller, Der Betrogene Patient, 'The Betrayed Patient.' This courageous doctor reveals why people are at risk when they seek medical treatment. Every year over 18,000 people die in German clinics because of medical errors. That is about five times as many deaths as in road traffic accidents. Dr Gerd Reuther, goes further claiming that there are considerable numbers of unreported deaths by doctors which would make this figure significantly higher.

Doctors who are true masters of health are scarce. Dr Buchinger was one of those, a man that inspired me to look at health in a logical but unconventional manner, he taught me how fasting heals. I was nineteen years old when I read his book about juice fasting. Inspired I followed his instructions closely, and fasted for six weeks, I never thought it would be possible, my first six weeks fast cleansed me deeply.

Stepping into Bravery

'The more you research the crazier you sound to Ignorant people,' Don Freeman

When we are faced with something we have not learned or cannot comprehend, we tend to dismiss it rather than embracing it as an opportunity to expand our understanding. Very few people question our government, media, scientists, financial institutions, or education system. If anyone dares to question anything, they get labelled as conspiracy theorists, or when people cannot find a logical explanation for something, they prefer to look the other way and then wonder why the country is ruled the way it is. Everyone who dares to question the storylines of the leading news channels is censored and defamed, highly qualified people such as award winning scientists, doctors, thinkers and some politicians are being scorned as conspiracy theorists. Why is there this shaming and undermining of people who suggest anything that goes beyond the narratives that are broadcast by the mainstream media? The media has skilfully directed our focus from one issue to another, we have been moved around the chess board by striking headlines at the press of a button. The world has gone from a deadly viral pandemic to the appalling game of racism whilst the masses follow failing to question their directives. Humanity has been brainwashed to believe there is a deadly disease spreading through the population by a barrage of daily news of vast quantities of people testing positive, and a daily death count read as if there is an Olympics competition for the most dead. Yet we do not see any evidence of this deadly disease in our neighbourhoods. What we do see is the disease of irrational fear.

We all have been witnessing how the media picks up one subject and spreads it like a wildfire, teaming up with celebrities to highlight their propaganda. To stir up fear and insecurity to control and manipulate for financial and political gain, if one needs to speak up about racial injustice, then why not speak up for all, all life should matter, otherwise there is no unity. So where are the headlines or press conferences that promote unity, self-empowerment, love, peace or independence and freedom?

Humanity has suffered as a whole, every race has been deprived throughout history to one extent or another, Injustice is running randomly through our society and history. Until today all sorts of people are suffering regardless of colour, the unjust cruelty that is committed to many children worldwide is the cruellest ordeal of all closely followed by poverty and famine in a world so rich in resources. Injustice affects the whole human race, not only one. Over eight million children go missing around the world every year. Yet it does not make the headlines. Ask yourself why?

Fear structures do not unite us, they will always separate us. We should Instead hold steady to our integrity and self-empowerment, the only way to honour unity is through love, care, and dignity, we do not have to sell ourselves to convince others we are equal, It is given that we are.

Those who follow blindly without thinking have fallen into a trap, making themselves pawns in someone's game, hiding behind the dictates of the media unwilling to take responsibility for their own decisions, accepting blindly what is dished up on the front cover of a tabloid or social media page endorsed by celebrities, that have fallen prey to the same control system. Celebrities are celebrities because of the media, their career entirely depends on headlines and promotions to sustain them. Like most of our politicians they also are the puppets of this grand controlling structure. If they do not play along, their careers will get negatively scrutinised by the media as we have witnessed many times.

Even scientific institutions have been compromised to project governmental agendas and have been used to slander or suppress alternative evidence based narratives. Most people neither have the means nor the drive to evaluate scientific evidence, therefore simply accept the declarations of politicised scientists which have been amplified by the mass media.

Everyone is waiting for someone to tell them the truth, the majority accept information delivered to them via the television as the only source of truth, but that is not how to find the truth. The truth is learned and discovered. If one cares for the truth, it takes effort to learn more than one narrative, to go beyond what has been whispered into one's ear. Go past the media, on a truth excursion, trace back all that is told, and do not be surprised to stumble on something you never expected, as truth is never told. It is learned.

'Every time I dig beyond what I had learned, my horizon widens to new possibilities.'

I came across many subjects that seemed doubtful, or made me feel uneasy, yet I still explored and educated myself in those matters. Investing in my consciousness remains the most valuable commodity, all it takes is time and willingness to expand one's perception. In the process, I acquired new knowledge and skills to distinguish deceptions that are circulated by our media and promoted by our governments. Knowing what I had learned made me feel freer.

'When history is distorted, changed or hidden, and information withheld, we as a humans are not able to alter our vibration.'

Yes, I had to first log in to empowerment and educate myself about many untouched or hidden subjects, and that took some training. Though while on the trail, I discovered many individuals and groups in the world that have been exploring topics our media or television channels never feature. Questionable projects that are kept from the public. I stumbled across scientists, researchers and historians with the most mesmerising discoveries presenting evidence of worlds other than ours, inhabited by advanced civilisations, and a past that is not as we have been taught to believe.

Those who go beyond the dictation of the government to tackle the truth are the real heroes of our time, it takes courage to go beyond the judgment of others, this bravery makes people unique.

Our bravery contributes to the raising of human consciousness. If we step into our powers, we cannot be controlled. We have a choice to bypass all of it by questioning and seeking answers within, to find the truth! This is when we reprogram our own subconscious mind, let's brainwash ourselves! Once we think, speak, and believe words of truth, we are changing our subconscious. Remember we are a sovereign beings and we have the power to achieve this.

When we step into our bravery, we are prompted to move away from ridiculous news that depicts events like cartoons where the villains become heroes, and turn the leaders in to followers. We will find something inspirational that is worthy of believing in.

Mind Control the Silent Weapon

But why we may ask? Implausible as it may sound, we all have been subject to human experiments, those capable of experimenting on animals are also capable of experimenting on humans, too much information has become available to be unaware of the social engineering that has been imposed and goes hand in hand with genetic engineering.

Mind control techniques are being applied to make it easier to control the human species, to edit the creative mind overwriting our natural belief systems to gain control over our biological and mental behaviour, in an attempt to compartmentalise our consciousness into a very limited frequency band, depriving us of knowledge, creativity and imagination. Every institution, organised structure and religion is responsible for this infringement.

To counteract free and open thought, all that is required is to gain control over the minds of the masses by promoting fear and helplessness, this is the agenda of social engineering, it is an attempt to break any links to our natural Earth, to higher knowledge, self-education or self-healing of the human body. Mass weather manipulation diminishes access to sunlight to create spiritual fragmentation. Our food contaminated with genetically modified organisms invade our bodies that lead to abnormal DNA plus artificial intelligence controlled programs that result in dysfunctional psychological behaviour.

Social media and mass media such as commercial television channels, printed and online newspapers control the mind with a goal to divide and vanquish any self-empowering belief, they serve an agenda designed to disempower.

Basically, this program serves to promote victimhood, when you are a victim, you are helpless and easier to control. These brainwashing tactics are silent weapons that are applied gradually so that we adapt obliviously to tolerate them. I believe ignoring everything that these channels of information are dishing up is the best thing one can do. This is exactly what I am doing, and it has served me well.

So many of us know and realise, that there is little sense in what our so called 'Leaders' present us with. This is the time for our awakening.

Awakening is accessing new knowledge, this is self-empowering, learning about the natural function of our bodies and reversing the brain washing programme that humanity has been subjected to.

Cognitive Dissonance

Every movie has a villain and a hero, many of us cheer for the hero who brings down the villain. It is ironic that millions of people love movies that depict heroic rebellions that resist oppression and fight for freedom and yet in everyday life they obey the rules of authority without questioning the justification, fairness, or integrity of those rules.

All that is required for a dominant entity to exist is for the masses to doubt its existence even when it is right under their noses in everyday life. The media have taken good care of it desensitising us to accept evil or control as normal. We do not realise that we are the saviours. Many believe that the extraordinary only occurs on their mobile screens. Whilst the mass media are busy promoting fear mongering stories and fake superstars, our real heroes are living amongst us right now, we have many individuals who do extraordinary heroic things every day without media coverage and do not ask for reward, true heroes who have no urge to tell a single soul.

How is it that domination occurs in the first place? It is the masses that are creating it, by accepting the programming that occurs every time they watch a movie depicting evil or corruption as part of everyday entertainment which leads to it becoming normalised. The absence of scrutiny creates mindless followers, allowing the controllers of the media to use them as their pawns. Just like dysfunctional relationships, no matter how obvious the proof presents itself many remain in disbelief even when their world is crumbling before their eyes.

Leon Festinger 1919–1989 was an American psychologist, who learned about a mental function known today as cognitive dissonance. He found that when deeply ingrain beliefs are challenged, a spontaneous resistance is created in the human mind. Leon Festinger's findings point to an installed function in the mind that holds on to a particular mindset which avoids deviation. People hold beliefs they associate themselves with, even if their beliefs are harmful or without benefit. The mind will simply resist any uncomfortable thought challenging their particular belief. This is known as the principle of cognitive dissonance. He further found when there is dissonance to dissolve to become free from the uncomfortable feeling, the belief pattern must also change to eliminate the dissonance. An adaptation in a person's mindset is required to reduce the discomfort and restore balance.

Our Ignorance Is Their Power

'Let's be enlightened by learning about everything they do. That will pull the rug from under their feet.'

There is more to the Universe than we will ever be capable of imagining. The more we become informed, the more we modify our frequency. When we collect truth data, our frequency raises, if we follow deception our vibration lowers. Most people follow what they are told, without question. Believing what they read or see in the news, as a result, they are unknowingly creating this reality themselves, unaware that they are being manipulated into believing lies.

Still a child in the seventies I remember watching on television a man named Stanley Meyer, who drove a car powered by water, it was a fully functioning car. He mysteriously died, his invention was slandered and vanished, although millions of us saw him driving that car. Meyer was a scientist that spent his entire life patenting innovative inventions. He was not the only one, looking into the life of the genius Nikola Tesla who had a similar ending. Nikola Tesla is the inventor of the Tesla Coil, a wireless energy device developed to provide free energy that was invented in 1891, why was this not developed? Is there something wrong with the history we were taught to believe? Why is it that so many scientists who attempted to develop free energy over the centuries mysteriously disappear? Are we deprived of technologies that already existed in the past? Why have certain revolutionary technologies not been developed? I remember as a little girl riding my bicycle that could power the front and backlights of my bike for free without using batteries. We also used calculators at school powered by solar power instead of batteries. Considering the advances, we have made today in technology, surely all mobile phones could be equipped to use some form of free solar energy by now? We are capable of powering houses and communities with solar panels, why not mobile phones? Why are energy supplies to our homes still provided by obsolete technology? How come most people still drive petrol cars while we have access to technology that is mind blowing, beyond most people's comprehension. Look at the software on our computers and devices. As a designer, I use various software. I work with highly intelligent technology that functions like magic powered from tiny crystal transmitters.

Why do we know so little about the history of Electric cars? TAMA is the name of an electric car that was developed in Japan by Tokyo Electro Automobile Co. Later It was renamed, Prince Motors Ltd. This car was first brought to the market in 1947 and then two years later in 1949 the same company rolled out an electric truck that could travel two hundred kilometres on a single charge. These developments took place during a time when Japan had a shortage of oil and so an alternative system of power was needed. During this period government incentives to achieve this caused a spike of new companies manufacturing electric vehicles. Strangely this clean energy concept was short lived.

Cars powered by electricity surprisingly were not new even in 1947. The first practical electric cars were invented and built prior to 1839. The concept was developed by Robert Anderson in Scotland and at around the same time by the American Thomas Davenport. The invention developed over the ensuing years and in 1897 electric taxis were introduced to the streets of New York and by 1900 almost a third of car production in America was electrically powered.

The polluting internal combustion engine was first introduced in 1885 by Karl Benz in Germany and the concept spread worldwide. If one compares the clean electric engine with the poisonous internal combustion engine it is strange how the latter gained precedence over the former. Today the most widely manufactured engines powering vehicles of all types are internal combustion engines. This infernal device uses technology that burns diesel or petrol is neither efficient nor clean, producing pollutants such as carbon monoxide, hydrocarbons, and nitrogen oxides. Noting how car and commercial vehicle design has progressed in all other areas, I wonder how on earth are we still stuck with such old technology that has polluted the planet for over a hundred years.

Unbelievable Turns Believable

'When the demons are real so must be the angels'

As I explored, I reached into the most magnificent place in the middle of which was hidden a quandary, I crossed with the darkness and the most dubious. While I was pondering the seemingly inconceivable brokenness and venality of the world, it was the whisper of my higher consciousness that salvaged my sanity.

'Do not try to figure everything out since it is incomprehensible, it is deep, it is vast, it is dark, and it is deceptive. Yet the darkness has to surface to be cleansed, this will lead to truth. What you are witnessing is humanity's great awakening, the collective transformation and ascension. There is no time of blame, nor space for revenge, as this will not free you, understand this is the time of change, freedom is ahead. You will need to leave the old behind to move forward. The truth can only exist because of deception and deception only exists because truth exists.' I expressed in my despair. 'How can I possible digest such insanity,'

'How many more components will it take you to accept that the darkness serves the light? and how many more experiences will it take you to face your fear of the dark? Information is light, without it, one is not able to evolve, one remains stuck in darkness. There will come a time when you will no longer need to seek information outside of yourself. Until then we will be with you to trigger you, creating sparks of light that allow the opening to create the raising of energy according to how much you are able to handle.

Becoming an impeccable curator of frequency is the highest aptitude of all, to be able to hold knowledge of the highest order inside yourself means being unlimited, as you become this, your frequency will then become available to all around you. Your ability to hold light is proportional to your bravery of being able to perceive the darkness. You are the light, and the dark is afraid of the light!'

With all that I had learned and discovered the good and deceitfulness, what could I do? I could deny it, and I could combat it, hold resentments, or live in fear. Ultimately, none of that held up or was satisfying, none of that would take me to a state I wanted to be.

'Our superpowers are to forgive, to love and to self-empower.'

We all have a superpower, and it is not our technologies. Freedom requires an ability to let go of all the beliefs that society has programmed into us. Decode any limiting beliefs programmed into us by the mainstream media, religious, education system, or any other cultural divisions. Love, forgiveness, and self-empowerment are our superpowers, this is our training, and this is what will release us and keep us free. Self-empowering is the key to freedom, accessing our powers means we discover who we are when we are empowered, when we love, when we let go, forgive, and become free from defence and take full personal responsibility for our own happiness, then there is no authority to blame. The ones that practise self-empowerment are their own authority and leaders and live as such. They do not see themselves as any less than God nor superior but equal, this is how we become free of dependency towards anyone.

We have access to our authenticity and unique skills, imagine a world where we are all geniuses. Everyone, with their own unique given sets of talents, shining in distinctive colours. Imagine how magnificent this will be, an environment where everyone thrives in their most authentic way marvelling at each other's talents.

'Happiness always leads to love and love is freedom. And when I feel free I can free others as only then will I truly know what freedom is'.

Before I Was Born

Ever since I can remember, I have felt intrigued to know where I came from, why I am here and how I came here. I had come across so many answers when I posed this question. One of the most common replies that I received was, 'I had a mission to accomplish,' or 'a lesson to learn dictated by God.' To add to my confusion, that 'mission', the one I had been born to accomplish, became yet another mystery to uncover. Somehow, I could not go along with those theories that some Godly being had sent me to this planet to comply with a mission that had been assigned to me, and if I do not fulfil this mission, what it was I had no clue, I would be consigned to some form of hell after death. I also contemplated the atheist's theory that we cease to exist after death. All of these ideologies seemed very restricting to me, they felt condemning and did not symbolise freedom, growth, joy or expansion. Needless to say, none of these answers satisfied me. Ever since during my early days of meditation when I had experienced myself in a bodiless state, I knew that my existence goes far beyond the physical.

My experiences widened my horizons and gave me access to thoughts and emotions of a higher level. The clarity that unfolded through my practises took me past my vision, it led me to access knowledge that lay beyond any doctrines or manmade ideologies. It was during meditation that I began to contemplate new ideas that led me to the neuroscience suggestion that we all are an extension of an infinite source of energy, connected to each other.

These ideas were contrary to what I had been taught as a BK whose ideology trained me to perceive myself separate from God and unworthy of him. Identifying myself as someone separate felt normal that was how I had always seen myself, as a singular being. In the beginning, my mind could not perceive the meaning of this expansive ideology of being an eternal being with an eternal connection and that we are all equal to God. I could not reach that meaning until one day when I had an experience. I was drifting deeper and deeper into a meditative state into a powerful bodiless sensation, I sensed a familiar presence within my consciousness, my curiosity triggered me to ask. 'Why can I not see you when I feel you so clearly?'

'No one is preventing you from seeing what you desire to see, you have sole ownership of your vision. Yet feeling things is also seeing, feeling things is seeing differently. You will always observe what is within your vision. Sometimes you cloud your vision with what you perceive as reality, or what everybody else thinks can or cannot be seen, then your vision cannot see beyond the material reality... come with me'

I felt gently pulled into a soft swirling pool of light spiralling me upwards. The swirling light had carried me into space where I had a full view of the Universe. *'Can you see now?'* I heard the voice ask. *'As you delve into the mysteries of the cosmos, you will construct a reservoir of knowledge readily available to draw upon when needed. As you gain this access to your mind, it will feel like you have tapped into a cosmic source of information.'*

I was looking down at the planet Earth. My vision had become like a telephoto lens. I could focus my sight, zooming in and out of various countries and cities, observing millions of people with colourful energy around them, constantly changing in colour as they moved around and performed various tasks. Large, colourful vibrational clusters would build where people were gathering, each colour representing a different frequency of energy, people matching those colours would be drawn to each other almost magnetically, finding their ways to exchange and play, they would move in and out of these various coloured energy islands. Sometimes the same people were drawn into other clusters where their vibration would change colour. Some people were very skilled as they were able to focus and move through these energy fields making their way to beautiful energy bundles. Others were somehow trapped, always emanating the same frequency and not moving beyond their standard coloured energy island.

Some vibrational clusters were immensely happy, exciting, fast, expansive and vibrant, others were less happy, moving at a lesser speed, while some were almost monotonous. Then there were the sad ones who were denser, duller in colour and heavier, experiencing life at its worst. There was no restriction as to who could access these energy clusters, it was all down to the individual's own vibrational frequency. *'Do you recognise them?'* The voice asked. Without awaiting my reply, *'Every single one of them is an individual manifestation of the same infinite intelligence. You are all interconnected beings, every person is a small element of a larger whole, an extension of infinite energy that has chosen to experience existence in a physical body on planet Earth. You chose this planet as you wanted to have the experience of Earth. You chose this life seeing this as a significant opportunity to experience something that you could only feel on Earth. Earth is this vast planet filled with so many opposing energies, you picked one of the most challenging planets that exists in the Universe. You knew you would experience contrast that would assist in your soul expansion and your mastery of freedom. And you took birth knowing that you would forget who you are and that you would experience separation and that is why you and every soul on this planet have guides to access your higher self to assist you and guide you through this experience of amnesia. When you do not maintain this connection to your guide you may find yourself looping in the same experience manifesting the same thing over again in different places with different people until the experience itself pushes you to go into yourself, that then catapults your next growth. It is pain that makes you ask for more freedom and when you start asking you start remembering, connecting to your guides to your higher self. They will support you in your shift to obtain your chosen desire.'*

As I was listening I started to perceive myself differently. Captivated by the words I was absorbing I blended with the wisdom they were projecting, thoughts were reverberating around me, like a tuning fork, I was finding my resonance. My mind became crystal clear, and an immense feeling of freedom passed through me. My perception of myself started to change. My mind was expanding. I was growing into this eternal being without a beginning or an end, and I was in a place of absolute understanding about who I was. I recognised myself as a bodiless form of energy with a distinct and independent existence, connected to a stream of wellbeing and love that could never be disconnected. I was feeling the deep connection I shared with all that existed in our world. I could remember my existence before my physical body formed in my mother's womb. I was the one who had chosen my parents, my body, my shape, and my looks. I had decided on it vibrationally. I had felt so deserving, virtuous and righteous to take my chosen birth, I had selected it as the foundation for my creation. I was aware of my ability to create and anchor light, I felt all knowing and all powerful, completely loved, safe and stable. Not for one moment did I doubt my potential or everyone else's capability to create.

I was drawn back to the voice and felt how it was addressing me with pure love. I could now see the shape of a magnificent celestial body, a beautiful and graceful humanly shaped silhouette made from the purest light moving in a divine motion.

'You are the creator of what you are seeing. Are you admiring your own beautiful creation or are you disappointed in what is manifesting around you?'

I heard the voice ask, it continued to speak without pause. *'Before you took birth, you understood that you are a creator, your task was to explore various levels of emotion and to expand consciousness on Earth. There is no Godly being that allocated a test or duty for you to fulfil while being in your bodily form, you came of your own free will, not to redeem yourself. You knew that it may be challenging, yet you still came and chose to assist this expansion, you are part of a universal transformation. Your planet Earth is also called Gaia, a living benevolent planet there is nothing to be fixed, there is only growth, your Gaia is ascending and so are you.'*

The voice started to slowly fade, and my mind was unable to hold on to the vastness of this divine intelligence that was softly moving away from me. I was trying to hold on to my position, but I could not and found myself being slowly drawn back into my present reality, in the room and the armchair I was in when I commenced meditation.

Brain Activation

'You and I are creators with access to a higher intelligence, a potent creative force, a stream of wellbeing that divinely appreciates everything that exists.'

Each feeling has frequency that shapes our world around us. Tuning in to the frequency of gratefulness creates a field of receptivity. It is a potent emotion. Creating thoughts intentionally requires practise. It can feel unnatural at the beginning, but with time, it becomes the most natural thing to do. I had many moments when I was trying to find something to be grateful for but couldn't get a whiff of it. Sure, it can be hard to transform undesirable situations, particularly when they are staring right in the face. The density of this low vibrational energy felt at times unmovable. It is a bit like being trapped in a downward emotional spiral. A negative momentum will not allow easy access to thoughts that feel good. The reason for this is that we only have access to ideas in the vibrational vicinity of our current emotions. We have to work ourselves up the ladder of emotion so to speak. At times like this it is natural to struggle. And struggle I did, though I had equipped myself with some tools for my rescue. I had to make magic happen through the power of my imagination. At my most desperate moments I kept asking myself,

'What would it take to transform this feeling to a better one right now,' and I would visualise, whatever positive idea I could grasp, over and over again until I felt the relief.

Real or imagined, our brain does not know the difference, we collect information through our senses and thoughts. The brain reacts based on the information we feed it, and it manages this information regardless of how it is received. The human brain does not distinguish between what is happening and what is imagined. It cannot tell the difference between something you are seeing, experiencing, or thinking. The brain will activate emotions in your body, regardless of how it received this information. If I imagine myself surrounded by people or an environment that genuinely appreciates me, I can sense a feeling of love and kindness, and an attitude of gratitude emerges. The brain receives this information as real. In my mind, I can dream up anything, and therefore transform anything. I am free to imagine the most significant and beautiful things.

Since we are only capable of holding one focus at a time whether it is a desired or undesired one we will move towards whatever we focus on. We are capable of great things when we apply our thoughts and emotions by dreaming and visualising a whole infinite world will open up to where everything one can think of exists.

Neuroplasticity

Our thoughts change the structure and function of our brain which has a fantastic ability to adapt and heal itself in response to any mental experience. Scientists recognise that the brain reorganises itself by forming new neural pathways throughout life. The mind is not fixed or unchangeable as was once thought. Our mind can create new neural pathways to adapt to its needs. The anatomy of the brain is made up of hundreds of billions of neurons, as well as trillions of support cells. Neurons are nerve cells that transmit signals to and from the brain, they are electrically stimulated cells that process and communicate information. Neurons are the most essential cells in the brain because they broadcast messages about what we are thinking, feeling or doing.

A neuron is a cell body also known as the soma, it has numerous dendrites which are the signal receivers. They are extensions of the cell body that appear like branches. Dendrite's function is to obtain information from other cells and carry that information to the cell body soma. The axons then carry a single signal from the soma to the target which is the next neuron or a muscle fibre. The axon is also known as nerve fibre, it is a portion of a nerve cell (neuron) that carries nerve impulses away from the cell body. The brain's reorganisation takes place by axonal sprouting, in which undamaged axons grow new nerve endings and connect with other safe nerve cells, forming new neural pathways, to accomplish a needed function. The brain can develop new pathways by having unique patterns of neural cells firing together as it is exposed to new information and environments. A saying that is commonly used by scientists is that 'neurons that fire together wire together.'

Whenever there are positive changes in behaviour patterns, environment, emotions, as well as repetitive positive thoughts or in general positive activity, we rewire our brain and strengthen the brain areas that stimulate positive feelings. Every time we learn something new, the brain creates new neural pathways. The more one focuses on and practises something, the better one becomes at the new skill.

One of the first scientists to be credited with the discovery of neuroplasticity was William James in 1890. He concluded that the brain is capable of 'reorganising itself by forming new neural pathways throughout life.' This idea, however, was dismissed at the time by a majority of scientists, who believed that the brain was fully developed at adulthood and specific regions were unable to change their function. Another misconception was that the human brain consists of 100 billion cells and that those cells die day by day and that we could not generate new ones. It was also believed that the brain could not create new neural pathways. All these beliefs have been proven wrong today. Neuroplasticity is one of the most critical developments in modern science's knowledge of the brain. Today the study of neuroplasticity has been furthered and we have a series of notable scientists, who believe that the brain is endlessly adaptable. They suggest that certain areas in the mind can generate fresh cells by focusing and repeating new thoughts, beliefs, and actions. This helps build new neural pathways which then become our ingrained habits.

This was something critical for me to understand. These discoveries were important and knowing this was invaluable and comforting and a way to bypass the mind manipulation structure we were subjected to.

London

I had not yet turned twenty years of age, when I made an impulsive decision to move to England, I said farewell to my then German boyfriend Stefan with the promise that I would return. Little did I know that London would become my new home, a platform and catalyst, leading me to the newness, the thrills and the secrets of life that I was seeking.

It took me some time to fall in love with London. There were moments when I would cry my eyes out, as I came up against challenges that only a fast city like London throws at you. London felt expansive, it gave me the feeling that everything was possible. It offered so much to explore, a city unlike any other.

My first fashion job was with Chelsea based couture designer Catherine Walker. I worked in an environment where visits from royalty and high society were the norm. I remember my first meeting with Princess Diana, her charisma was immediately evident, she was radiant and charming. I hadn't been particularly a fan of her until this point. I remember being captivated by her kind and playful aura that I felt radiating of her, it made her immensely attractive, whatever this energy was that flowed so effortlessly through her, it felt magnetic which I can still recall today. I understand why people were so quickly drawn to her. None of the other royals that walked through the doors of our design studio felt quite as captivating. No matter how glamorous my encounters were. 'I often caught myself pretending to enjoy them'. Somehow, the 'celebrity prominence' did not feel quite as satisfying as I had imagined. There was more I was desiring and longing for, there were still many questions to be answered for.'

London was cosmopolitan, and I would meet people from many diverse backgrounds. I was always fascinated by their different traditions and beliefs. As time passed, I started to feel more and more comfortable in the great city of London. I would meet thinkers and visionaries, people with great abilities who would pass through or stay in London, some wiser than others. I had access to so much information and learning. I was fascinated and drawn to people with exceptional minds, and I was intrigued by fresh and new ways of thinking. I discovered different cultures, beliefs, and spiritual practices such as meditation. Whilst one would imagine that meditation is something to explore only deep in the Himalayas, I collided with it right in the core of the bustling city of London.

My curiosity about meditation kept growing, it turned out to be a fantastic tool to let creativity flow. I taught myself meditation from books as at the time the internet was not as sophisticated as today. Since I did not know anyone who meditated, I bought several books about Buddhism, Hinduism, and Feng Shui. These books taught me about the art of vibrations and explained the energy we project and the effect it has on our lives. I could not quite grasp all of the ideas I was presented with but I was excited to discover many things I had not previously known. I started experimenting with the various ideas I had discovered with my extensive reading. I practiced focused meditation and found that my senses felt heightened. I began to discern the subtle energies my body was projecting. I started to experiment with my hands, using them to feel the energy of the plants, walls and the other objects around my home. I had no idea whether I was doing it right, but I could feel things. Guiding myself through different techniques, checking which one felt the best. With regular practice, I developed an ability to sense the energy in my surroundings more clearly. I was intrigued by my discovery and burned with desire to know more.

I wanted to upgrade my life and create a pure energy space. In order to tune in more easily and have access to higher frequency space, I started to cleanse my space at home. Our home's surroundings are an extension of ourselves, once we let go of old stuff, we create space for newness in our lives. I never was a big fan of accumulating things yet somehow, I had still gathered many unneeded possessions. My instinct told me to rid myself of clutter. When I read about Feng Shui I was instantly attracted by the idea of clearing space, to make room for newness. It was eye opening to learn how things kept around us shape our lives.

When I feel Intrigued about something I explore intensely and become inspired, I read several books about Feng Shui, took instructions, and began my experiment of how to rid my home and life of things that do not serve me. I did a thorough cleansing of my home, throwing out everything I had not used during the past six months. I cleaned every single drawer, got rid of old cutlery and odd non matching kitchenware then replaced items where required. I went through all my photos throwing out all of the duplicates or the ones that carried sad memories, keeping only those that carried happiness. I rid myself of any belongings that felt sad. I went around each room ringing a Tibetan Buddhist bell and throwing salts to clear trapped energy. This thorough clean out took me five full days and it was only a small one bedroom flat.

After I had finished clearing unwanted negative belongings and memories, I filled the space with love. As a part my plan I wrote a letter to myself of all the things I wanted to fill my new life with, the things I wanted to achieve and create within the next year. I sealed the letter and locked it in a pretty box and promptly forgot about it.

The most unexpected thing happened immediately. I lived in a house that had four flats, each of my neighbours started clearing their clutter too, and before I knew it we all had crystals hanging on our front doors. Visitors said how beautiful my home looked and felt, although it was a small and basic flat, nothing impressive, the energy had changed and created a beautiful living space that reached the whole house. I had changed my living space and my life also started to reform, out of nowhere new people appeared with similar interests to mine. Those were the people, the teachers, and friends I had asked for in my letter. My life transformed. I created an entirely new world around me, a new circle of friends and acquaintances evolved very quickly.

When years later I came across my pretty box with the sealed letter written to my future self, it was extraordinary to read what my younger self had written. I was amazed looking at those words from so long ago. All I had committed to paper It had actually been realised.

Tuning to a Higher Intelligence

Meditation remains one of the most essential tools in my life, helping me to not only maintain my mental stability during difficult times but also to increase my awareness and appreciation of the exciting and happy moments in my life. It can be described as tuning into a source of energy that is incredibly wise, inspiring and all knowing. When I first started practising meditation, I could barely sit still for five minutes but I was determined to master the art so I practised daily for six months until I was able to reach a deep state of stillness within myself and began to feel the positive effects of meditation. The words and explanations I had read did not do justice to what I was discovering.

In the following years I deepened myself awareness and my experiences gradually became more unusual and rewarding. I was overcome by feelings of euphoria, a deep belonging, a connection to extreme love and encounters with divine intelligence. These experiences were deeply intoxicating and at times it was hard to return to reality. I would lose myself completely meditating for hours, going beyond this physical world to where I found myself in timeless realms. Once my mind had stretched to accommodate this new knowledge, it could never regain its previous status, there was no way back, only a gradual expansion to reach an ever higher level.

There are many forms of meditative exercises, whilst a BK, I was taught to meditate with my eyes open, it meant I was able to achieve a state of soul consciousness in any circumstances without the need to close my eyes. I was focusing inwards visualising a point of light, this focus slowed my thoughts to create a state of stillness, a state of timelessness, peacefully dwelling in divine love, and then there were those moments of feeling limitless. I was not actively using my thoughts during this state, creating thoughts with intention through internal focus was not part of the BK studies which was something I learned and understood much later.

I experimented with several types of meditational practices. The most empowering was the practice of limitlessness. I do not see meditation as clearing the mind, but more as focusing into the source light which slows and transforms my thoughts. This union is a realigning and tuning to my higher being, to receive ideas and impulses. Whilst experimenting with various ideas, I developed my own personal way of refocusing myself into alignment with my higher self, our minds are limitless, I was stretching my horizons to line up energies, that allowed the receiving of new thoughts. One may like to think of it as a reboot of new programming.

We are only thoughts away from our desires, feeding the mind is like feeding the body, all that is put in, will express itself outwards. I really like deep thought and I also love having my own space to create. In this space of self-care, inspiration flows with ease, as there is no one to judge and creation just happens, instinctively and naturally. Often, I get questioned, 'how can you spend so much time by yourself?' This is because people do not comprehend the satisfaction I experience when I make space to focus and create. Each one of us processes stimuli via different pathways in our brains, meaning we are all different in how we stimulate and respond to our senses.

For example, someone who gets excited being around lots of people is sometimes considered an extravert. By contrast, I could be described as an introvert. I am not keen on labelling myself in any way, as I am also very capable of enjoying myself by being around people. I likewise love spending time on my own to recharge, learn new things, or experiment with new ideas. I like to focus on finding a space to be with myself, contemplating or entertaining great ideas in my mind. It feels exciting and uplifting and brings solutions as to how I can make things better.

I easily perceive the mental and emotional waves of another individual, having people around all the time can interfere with my creative energy. This can feel uncomfortable since their energies are often not resonating with me. I find myself being moved away from such environments particularly when they are of lower frequencies, the circumstances always arrange themselves in such a way that I find myself working on my own or with small groups of very focused people. Our minds are meant to focus, I use meditation to go deep into my mind, what I experience during this time of focus often goes beyond my own expectations. I can direct my focus sharply during this quiet time, when I do this, I make my brain spark in new ways, which creates new experiences that help me to build and sustain new ideas. I am sometimes asked how I meditate and what I feel or see, but words can never provide the true expression of my experience. If one truly wants to know what it is like, one has to discover it for oneself.

Let's Meditate

When preparing for meditation I always ensure that I sit comfortably so my body does not distract me. I like to sit cross legged leaning my back on to a large cushion against a wall or relax into an armchair. I start with focusing on the centre of my forehead, visualising a beam of light entering through the crown of my head, spreading through my entire body. This sensation soothes me, and I begin to relax, my thoughts start to slow down, and I notice how delicious it is to breathe. I breathe in deeply to exercise my lungs which expand and pump oxygen into my blood stream. This gives me a deep sense of satisfaction and I relax more deeply. I continue my focus to the centre of my forehead. I focus internally visualising myself as a point of light that consists of pure, powerful and positive energy. I feel tiny muscles flexing in my face and body stimulated by the energy flow I am drawing in.

I sit still deepening this awareness until it feels stable enough. It then naturally expands itself further, I become that point of light sitting right in the centre of my forehead, powerful, peaceful, divine and stable. I visualise a stream of light pouring from the universe into the crown of my head which continues straight through my body connecting me to the core of the Earth. I merge with the light, I am the light, and the light is me. At this deep state, I am in a state of learning. I get to understand who I am and what my body is. My beautiful and luminous body is pure perfection, every cell, every sense is perfect and intelligent. My cells are smart and have their own way of recuperating. At times, my body feels almost separate from me, but then we are one again. I feel clear minded and every question I ask is answered almost instantaneously. Immersed in this positive atmosphere, I feel empowered and wonder why on Earth I have ever worried about anything. Worries, at this moment, seem pointless, I feel fresh, eager and clear.

I start to understand with a broader capacity, how emotions develop, as a result of the chemicals my body releases, related to the beliefs I hold. Which I can modify at will, turning negative thoughts to positive, so that my body can become receptive to all sorts of wonderful emotions created within.

Silent Senses

At the height of my time with the Brahma Kumaris, I travelled to Italy to attend a seven day silent retreat. The Gubbio Retreat Centre run by the BKs was tucked away in the beautiful hills of Umbria the air pure and clean and surrounded by natural lakes and lush verdant countryside. A group of about thirty BKs had joined together to observe seven days of silence. I arrived one day late as I had missed my flight. The silence had already commenced, no one was allowed to speak or write except the residents, and only minimally. We were all assigned duties to support the smooth running of the retreat. My assignment was to assist the head chef, a BK brother, in the kitchen to prepare meals for the group.

I had never worked in a kitchen or met this BK brother before, it was an encounter of silence. It was my first experience being involved in preparing three meals a day for so many people. On the first day, the chef took a notepad and wrote down the instructions for me to read. As the menu changed daily so new instructions would need to be given. On the second day, before he could pick up his pen, I intuitively started doing the things before receiving his written instructions. In surprise he broke the rules and whispered, *'How did you know?'* Somehow, I just knew precisely what he wanted me to do. I even learned how to make bread using the kneading machine and the baking oven and other tasks I had never carried out before, all without a manual or words. A perfect coherent working routine developed in that kitchen without words, other helpers joined us at intervals to assist with the dishes and the clearing up and everyone knew their tasks. It became an enchanted working environment, a silent dynamic that involved a sense of fun without engaging in words. A bustling kitchen running perfectly without speaking, until the last day when silence was broken.

Seven days had passed. I was talking again for the first time and it felt somehow exciting. We all had developed a sisterly and brotherly bond even though we had not spoken before. On the last day of our silent retreat the instructions were given to me in spoken words. It felt like a disorientation we kept bumping into each other, I misunderstood instructions and nearly caused an accident. There was a moment when I stopped and laughed saying, *'Can we please go back to being silent in this kitchen?'*

When our minds are still, a form of telepathy becomes natural and we are able to receive the thoughts of others. This is our inbuilt intuition and natural way of being, we all have this ability.

Creativity

We have adopted so many misconceptions about Godhood which has muddied the knowledge that we ourselves are Gods. Within the universes live many intelligent beings, souls that evolved over time and advanced their capabilities to attend to their aspirations and express themselves creatively. The significance of existence and consciousness is creativity and creativity take many forms.

I have felt irritated by people who tried to emulate my behaviour pattern or agree with every idea or action I take with no opinion or inspiration of their own. I wished them to be their authentic self, to feel independently inspired and most of all to be true to themselves. I shall always hold this wish for all.

Authenticity keeps us creative. Creativity is natural and unique and not something I would force to happen. I allow myself to receive the ideas, suggestions and inspirations through my alignment with my higher being. I let the thoughts, words, images, and impulse flow to me. Everyone of us has at some stage experienced this open mode, the point when we feel the perfection of our ideas.

Evolution and expansion are the makeup of our universe. We are always striving for improvement. This is a natural part of us that cannot be stopped no matter what. Everyone who conveys thoughts, feelings, words, or gestures is an innovative creator. Those that strive to use their learning and intuition in a creative and expanding way are fulfilling their desires. Not only artists, singers, and writers are creative people, but also everyone who uses their intuition combined with their learning. Sportsmen working on techniques, mothers and fathers who must adapt continuously require creativity, those people that use their own creative thinking to stimulate innovative ideas and findings will live satisfying lives. Today, I primarily see everyone as an artistic creator, with endless opportunities.

The best inspiration is alignment. Alignment will guide us. I am constantly overflowing with ideas with a mind that is full of countless visualisations and concepts. How is it that so many believe that our inspiration is limited? For myself, creativeness was never a sporadic experience, but abundantly, endlessly available, it would carry me to the right places.

Our nature is to be creative, creation starts with thoughts that trigger emotions and our actions follow based on how we think and feel. Undeniably my best ideas come to me when I am feeling good, this is when I become receptive to my higher life force, an alignment that makes my creativity spark. We all have the potential to glide through life to live those moments when everything works out effortlessly, ideas flow with ease, life feels enchanted and exciting, and a sea of opportunities appear right in front of us readily available to step into.

Each of us is unique and equipped with unlimited ideas and ready to bring them into this world. Listen to your inner guidance. It knows the way, pause, pay attention whenever you are in doubt. An unhindered mind vibrates in a frequency that will tap into those universal records to draw the required thoughts to make things happen. We are beings with bodies that can be utilised like supercomputers, a creative, magnificent machine that responds to our intentions and consciousness.

When we form a thought in an attempt to create something, it is not that we are inventing something, as everything already exists universally, we are merely tapping into this universal library. Our platform is the drawing board that we operate from, and we choose accordingly in order to live out a specific experience.

If I am searching for data in my mind, I am tuning my thoughts like the strings of an instrument which have a certain frequency. Those vibrational frequencies grant me access to this universal library, our galactic internet so to speak. Also known as the Universal Akashic Records. This is a compilation of all past, present and future thoughts and emotions experienced by souls.

Everyone has rightful access to these chronicles which contain templates for human ideals. Tuning into the Akashic Records provides endless inspiration ready to be received.

When the Path Bends

How do you drift into a monastic form of life, one that is disciplined and controlled and involves living under vows?

Still in my late twenties, I found myself lost without a real direction as how to shape my life. I was having lunch with my friend, Ingrid at her home in Kensington, when I first heard about a group of mysterious sisters, dressed in white that hosted private meditation sessions from an apartment in Mayfair, the gatherings were by invitation only. My friend Ingrid was an accomplished artist, originally from Austria and lived with her family in the Albert Mansions Kensington. Ingrid had an attractive and charming personality, we had met several months earlier during a visit to Harrods. Part of Ingrid's art was inspired by her spiritual encounters. I loved Ingrid's company, she was wise, fun, easy going and loving, with a generous heart. We always had exciting conversations about art, spirituality and life. I enjoyed listening to her and found her stories courageous and inspiring.

Some years ago, she had been diagnosed with cancer and had been given six months to live. I was fascinated to learn how she had managed to make her tumour disappear through a series of self-healing practices and focused meditation. It not only extended her life but enacted a complete change of lifestyle. Ingrid appreciated my newfound interest in meditation that I was exploring at the time. She had told me about the sisters on numerous occasions, and I had become increasingly curious. I agreed to join her at their next meeting.

A small group of us arrived at the apartment in Mayfair. I was excited and curious to finally meet the sisters. The apartment was in a prestigious block and was owned by one of the sisters. On arrival, we were asked to take off our shoes before entering the space. I took off my shoes and positioned them neatly onto the shoe rack situated by the entrance. Barefoot I stepped through the open door onto a spotless glossy wooden floor. The residence was an open light space, decorated with minimalistic contemporary white furniture and parts of the walls had modern fresco artworks painted directly on them which were pastel portraits of graceful angelic beings.

'Welcome to my home,' I was greeted by a beautiful woman with glowing eyes and a beaming smile, 'I am Maryam,' she said. Maryam was a *'pakka'* surrendered sister, a Brahma Kumari. She was beautiful, smart and well educated, from a prestigious family background. I later discovered Maryam had been practising meditation since her teenage years.

I was led into a large living area which had a calm atmosphere, a small group of us sat comfortably on cosy sofas and armchairs ready to begin the meditation session. Maryam explained that this practice is called Raja Yoga. The BK's version of Raja Yoga is not related to the traditional Raja Yoga. It does not involve any breathing exercises or specific body postures or other rituals, but the central aspect is to focus to gain control of the mind. Yoga means 'linking', 'Raja' means King. This means linking with the King or God. The aim is union with the divine through a process of spiritual purification. After our first meditation session, I was invited to return and join further classes.

Enticed by my first encounter, I kept going back for more. I would visit Maryam regularly to study the foundations of 'Raja Yoga meditation,' Maryam and I bonded like sisters, it felt satisfying to study under her guidance.

One evening Maryam invited me to join a talk hosted by the BK at Kensington Town Hall. The talk was led by one of India's most renowned spiritual leaders, Dadi Janki. The class was fully booked, with every seat occupied and many more standing. I had met Dadi in a private gathering at Maryam's apartment on two previous occasions. Dadi Janki had a powerful presence, a renowned globally recognised spiritual leader who was also Maryam's spiritual mentor. Dadi Janki was woman in her late eighties at the time with clear sparkling hazel eyes and a captivating energy, little did I know that Dadi would become one of my closest spiritual mentors for the next seven years.

Dadi gave an inspiring talk, captivating each of us with her wisdom, Dadi always spoke in Hindi, her words were translated into English as she spoke by her interpreter a young BK sister dressed in a white uniform who sat beside her.

Just before the class came to an end, Dadi addressed all visitors through her translator asking, 'Who would like to commit to a study of daily early morning meditation? It will be provided free of charge.' I enthusiastically put my hand up, I felt curious to explore a routine of regular early morning meditation, I had wished for some sort of support group. I was seated in the front row and saw Dadi observing the room, and after a pause, she spoke again, 'Very often people do not understand the value when there is no price attached to it. I looked around, and I saw I was the only one who had put my hand up.

Immediately after the event, I was called to see Dadi Janki. Maryam joined me while Dadi asked me some personal questions and then arrangements were made so that I could attend the early morning meditation classes at the London headquarters of the Brahma Kumaris Spiritual University. Maryam was assigned to be my immediate teacher and to report my progress directly to Dadi. Over the next seven years, Maryam and Dadi Janki mentored me through my studies, training me how to be a *'pakka'* (proper) Brahma Kumari sister. From that day, I did not miss one class for the next seven years; an intensive discovery of elation and conflicts unfolded in front of me.

During the first weeks, I was taught what it meant to be a *'pakka'* Brahma Kumari yogini sister. Brahma Kumari translates as 'daughters of Brahma.'

The founder, Brahma Baba, was a wealthy jeweller in India, he gave exceptional importance to the role of women, who have come to play prominent roles in the organisation which consists of over 8,500 centres, in more than 100 countries. Brahma Baba stood up for equality and empowerment of women in India. The status of women in India during the twentieth century was far from satisfactory, men and husbands traditionally held authority over women who were often isolated and mistreated by them.

Brahma Baba used his wealth to create a campus, a space where mistreated and abused women could find sanctuary, they were educated and trained to hold prestigious roles as leaders within the institution.

I had not yet grasped the status of Dadi Janki and the important position she had gained as a spiritual leader and representative of the BK. Dadi had been one of the selected disciples who had trained directly with the founder Brahma Baba in 1937. When I met her, she was one of the leading figures and the administrative head of the Brahma Kumaris.

Who Was Dadi Janki?

Life is full of mystery and so was my encounter with Dadi Janki, her aura certainly emanated a powerful authority, an energy that felt captivating, there was a sense of comfort when near to her.

An aura is an energy field which each one of us projects. A strong aura is captivating, it allows us to attain higher states of consciousness. Anyone that is fine tuned to draw in high frequency light obtains a powerful aura and can share their energy which travels to the weaker recipient raising their vibratory rate. Those who are receptive will feel a rise in frequency, some also experience phenomena such as spiritual experiences and healings. When we feel vulnerable, we vibrate at a low level, therefore can easily be seduced or impressed by someone that vibrates higher. Of course, this is only until we rise above. This is when we experience our own powers.

Dadi Janki died on the 27 March 2020 aged 104 in Mount Abu. This was after I had left the Brahma Kumaris institution. I am still mystified today, by her presence and teachings. What was her true role? Could I understand it or was it beyond my capacity to comprehend in this dimension? Have I allowed myself to have been misled and hypnotised or was this woman the 'saint' as I had believed? Was I being groomed for a higher purpose, or was my experience with a structure organised to sustain a spiritual institution? This remains an enigma.

Dadi would often share her childhood memories with us. Dadi Janki was born as Janki Kripalani in 1916 into a Sindhi family at Hyderabad in the northern Indian province of Sindh which is now in Pakistan. Her exact date of birth is unknown as no birth certificate exists. She only obtained a passport much later in life and for the purpose of issuing that passport her birthday was given as the 1st of January 1916. The young Janki spent much of her time on pilgrimages in her search for truth, she was a dedicated vegetarian and educated her community about the health benefits of a vegetarian diet. When she was still a teenager, she would take her father's horse and carriage to travel around her neighbourhood visiting the elderly with who she would often stay to give love and comfort.

As a young woman Janki refused the Indian custom of arranged marriage. Although the story is unclear, Dadi was raped resulting in her becoming pregnant. Very little is known about her child. Dadi would often share her stories with us during class but would never give any details of her pregnancy or the resultant child.

Dadi suffered many childhood illnesses, her body was often in pain to such an extent that even a breeze brushing by her skin would cause her agony. Yet Janki taught herself to rise above her misfortune. During the years I knew Dadi Janki, she fell ill from time to time but never neglected her duty to conduct a class. She often spoke of the art of overcoming physical pain.

Still in her youth Janki had a series of visions that guided her to seek her way to Bhai Lekhraj who today is known as Brahma Baba the founder of the Brahma Kumaris. She spent only three years in formal education before joining the Brahma Kumaris boarding school. Aged twenty-one in 1937 Janki joined what was then referred to as the Yagya institution, known as the BKWSU today.

Bhai Lekhraj [Brahma Baba], the founder of BKWSU was a man who broke down adherence to the caste system that prevailed in India and provided support to Indian women who had been undermined and disadvantaged for many generations. He set up a boarding school for young women also run by women, which provided formal education and spiritual training. Bhai Lekhraj faced many adversities and legal challenges for going against the traditional system.

Another personality in Dadi Janki's development was Radhe Pokardas Rajwani who at twenty two years old also found her way to the founder Bhai Lekhraj and his institution. Radhe visited the institution attending meetings and meditation practice. After three years her abilities flourished. This young woman was destined to play a unique and important role within the Yagya institution (BKWSU) she was appointed as the President of the institution in 1937 and remained in this post until her passing in 1965.

When the institution was legally challenged, the remarkable Radhe represented the institution in court, with a maturity and grace of a living goddess and was recognised as such amongst the Brahma Kumaris. Radhe became known as Om Radhe and was also referred to as the Spiritual Mother or simply Mamma.

Mamma assembled a management committee made up of eight selected women who were known to have been led to the institution through divine guidance. The eight leaders of the Yagya institution were groomed to become the leaders of the BKWSU and are today known as the Dadis of the original Yagya institution. Out of the original eight, three are still alive and remain the leaders of BKWSU. They are Dadi Hirdaya Mohini, known as Dadi Gulzar, which means rose garden, Dadi Ratan Mohini and Dadi Ishu. I was privileged to meet and study with them during my visit to Mount Abu.

Dadi Janki was one of the eight although she had joined the others a year later, she immediately dedicated her life to the studies. Mamma became the direct mentor to Dadi Janki. Brahma Baba also played a significant role in Dadi's spiritual evolution. She received many written guidelines unique to her from Brahma Baba. In 1969 Brahma Baba passed away, four years after Mamma.

Dadi Janki being one of the elders was appointed to take on leading responsibilities in running the intuition. Although Mamma and Brahma Baba had left their physical bodies, they subsequently started to make telepathic contact initially through various channels within the institution and ultimately through Dadi Gulzar who became the exclusive channel for transmitting their messages and the Murli. The Murli is the name of the channelled teachings transcripts.

The institution expanded nationally and in 1974 Dadi Gulzar channelled messages from Brahma Baba instructing Dadi Janki to travel to London to found the first international Brahma Kumaris centre. Dadi was initially hesitant to travel to London as she did not speak English, yet she did travel and took a sister who would translate when she conducted classes. I remember Dadi Janki sharing the story of her arrival in London. She and a small group of Brahma Kumaris initially lived in a small flat in Kilburn sharing a kitchen with others in a non-vegetarian household. Beginning with only a handful of followers, Dadi Janki established the London Brahma Kumaris centre which was the first to open in Europe. The Brahma Kumaris centres have grown considerably since this single outpost and today have established institutions in one hundred and forty countries worldwide.

The Seductive Disciplines

The BK Spiritual University headquarters in London was a contemporary, spotless, massive building with various study rooms and a large auditorium where regular classes and lectures were held. My duty was to follow all of the disciplines in order to be allowed to join regular morning classes and visit BK retreats. According to the BK, it was vital to follow those disciplines to maintain a pure vibration in the classrooms and centres around the world.

My curiosity was endless, and my sense of adventure made it natural to commit. Maryam was responsible for explaining the disciplines and meanings and guiding me through to the fulfilment of them to be a Brahma Kumari who becomes pakka by following all instructions accurately. Pakka is a word used within the BK community that translates into firm or proper in following the BK's code of conduct which serves to keep the mind in an elevated state.

The daily routine of a BK starts at 4:00am in the morning with a meditation practice known as Amritvela for a minimum of thirty minutes. This is considered the most potent time, forming the basis of being a Brahma Kumari and should never be missed, not even during illness. A Brahma Kumari always meditates with eyes open, to cultivate the habit of tapping into soul consciousness at any time. The aim is to spend all of our time in the consciousness of being a soul even while performing other tasks.

After the morning meditation is private study time as part of the routine before attending class at 6:30 to 8:00am. At 6:30am it is the time when all BK students come together in the auditorium for collective meditation. Afterwards everyone attends to their daily duties, stopping at hourly intervals for five minute meditation breaks throughout the day. In the evening at 7:00pm, the BK students gather again for collective meditation.

I struggled to wake up or even stay awake for the 4:00am meditation. My first few attempts to awaken failed. I fell straight back to sleep, feeling annoyed each time that I missed it. I truly wanted to know what it would feel like to meditate at this time as I had heard the most intriguing stories. This time was not only crucial to the BK but was also to the World's doctrines for meditation, and prayer. All sorts of spiritual believers would use this time for their religious practises and prayers thus creating a powerful collective atmosphere across countries, continents and the World.

Maryam suggested that I instruct my mind before going to sleep to ensure I wake up at 4:00am, this was supposed to help. On my fourth attempt, as suggested, I asked my mind to ensure that I woke up at 4:00am. I fell asleep and a few hours later, I was awoken by a loud, old fashioned alarm clock, ringing uncomfortably loud into my ear. The ringing made me jump, I had heard the sound coming through the pillow though there was no alarm under my pillow, and it was not my mobile alarm which I had forgotten to set. I could not explain what had happened or see any evidence of where such an old fashioned ringing sound could possibly have come from. I could have sworn what had awoken me was the ringing of a real old clock. Had I dreamed it?

I sat up in my bed to start my meditation. Although it is not advisable to meditate in bed to avoid snoozing off again. However I felt alert and eager so I positioned myself in a comfortable upright cross legged pose to start my first 4:00am meditation.

A strongly charged energy pulled me instantly into a bodiless state, 'Wow', I thought, this time of the morning indeed was powerful. The next thing I knew I found myself floating on the ceiling of my bedroom, not quite comprehending how it had happened. I could see my body sitting on my bed, I was looking down at myself, I panicked, and was pulled straight back into my body. Utterly perplexed by what had just happened, I then understood that it was an out of body experience.

This profound experience was vivid and exhilarating enough to make me eager to awaken very early the following days. My 4:00am practises that followed were heartfelt and beautiful. However tired I felt in the day, I followed my routine dutifully every morning at 4:00am, although I found myself falling asleep at my worktable in broad daylight. As my meditation became more concentrated, I became less interested in sleeping, my body adjusted to the early hours and soon it felt natural to wake up and I learnt to power nap if needed, to deal with the daytime tiredness .

Cleanliness Is Godliness

'The BK follow strict hygiene protocols,' I was told by Maryam. It felt satisfying when I was taught about the high standards of hygiene that had to be followed as part of the BK disciplines as I was someone who treasured cleanliness.

'Everyone is expected to shower each morning before class, wear a fresh set of clothing daily, and shower in the evening before going to sleep. After using the loo, one must shower, and change clothes again, if this is not possible then take your clothes off before the bathroom, shower after using the loo and then put them back on. The reason for this is that while the body passes solid waste during a bowel movement, it also expels toxins through the *skin's pores.'*

Food preparation was also a unique process. It was explained that food affects human consciousness. What we eat will change our way of thinking and feeling. I had always been conscious of what I was eating and intuitively avoided eating garlic and onion because of their unpleasant odour. However, I was learning entirely new ideas about food. *'A Yogi eats only pure food, and what is termed as pure food depends on how and by who the food is prepared. Our bodies are to be nourished with a pure vegetarian diet, prepared only by a BK.'* This meant no eggs, or very hot spices, which were considered harmful stimulants also no garlic, leeks, shallots or other plants belonging to the onion family which are considered to have a negative influence on our mind, slowing down our concentration and dimming our pineal gland. In addition Brahma Kumaris do not smoke, take drugs or consume alcohol. They do not eat the flesh of animals since the slaughtered animals carry extreme traumatic vibrational influences developed during the suffering and stress inflicted in the slaughterhouse. The animal releases stress hormones and that negative energy is impregnated into the flesh, if consumed it compromises our natural values. The BKs put a strong emphasis on vibrational influences. We studied vibrational transformation and were taught that undesired low frequencies may sway the soul's focus pulling it back to a denser state of mind. Hence the energy we consumed to fuel our bodies had to be pure and carefully selected.

A Brahma Kumari should not consume food prepared by someone impure, that is anyone who does not follow equal disciplines to the BK. This in practice meant that we would not eat food prepared by anyone outside of the BK, so no restaurants, coffee shops, take aways or external parties. In the event of finding ourselves in an environment where pure food was not available, we would eat fresh fruit or vegetables which did not require preparation.

The BKs follow a vegetarian diet as opposed to a vegan diet which in my opinion contradicts their doctrine, which is about animal welfare and a high frequency diet. The suffering caused by dairy production is certainly not something I would conceive as high frequency diet. This was a hypocritical doctrine that I pointed out but no logical answer was ever given.

Preparing meals was a sacred event, it had to be conducted in silence, in a meditative state so as to not pollute the meal with any unpleasant thoughts whilst in preparation. On occasion I would help in the kitchen to prepare meals. There were a further set of rules required to be adhered to. Prior to entering the kitchen, I had to shower and change into a fresh set of clothing so as to not carry any undesirable energy that I may have picked up outside that could contaminate the food preparations or the kitchen space.

Once the meal had been cooked it would also undergo a purification offering before serving. This is done by placing samples of the prepared meal into small containers on a tray. The tray is then covered with a delicate piece of cloth and placed on a raised platter in front of a group or an individual, to be offered to God through meditation with the request to have the prepared food cleansed and energised. Following the purification offering the food samples would then be mixed back into the main meal so that the vibration of the purified and charged samples could spread throughout the entire preparation. Finally, when the meal was served before eating, each BK personally charged the meal on their own plate by giving it Drishti and cleansing it further.

The Spiritual Vision Drishti

Drishti is frequently used by the BK. Drishi is a charged gaze, an internal focus or activation of the third eye. That can be directed at an object or person. Amongst the BK we used Drishti as a greeting or as an exchange of affection by gazing from soul to soul via the 'third eye.' BKs are taught not to hug or touch, but to use Drishti as a form of energy exchange to express love. With practice one can attain a stable, sovereign, and powerful vision, it builds up over time as one masters how to draw in benevolent light or other forms of energy that linger in the atmosphere. It can be used as a divine tool or for manipulation and can be very hypnotic. It is an ideal tool to trap and brainwash the unwary and without doubt it had misuse within this organisation. At the time I was not aware it could be misused. I would be very receptive and receive Drishti frequently, knowingly and unknowingly, which is perhaps the reason why I became so intensely entranced.

The dress code of a Brahma Kumari is always white, to symbolise purity, and to be easily identified, the same dress code applies in all the BK centres around the world for the male and the female. BKs are referred to as sisters and brothers, strict celibacy is observed, with no form of intimacy, bodily contact or touching of fellow yogis or any other people. The BK hold the belief that sensual pleasure blunts the intellect. They also suggest sensual pleasure leads to sorrow or jealousy which can interfere with one's focus and vibrations. Attachment can also lead to sorrow, therefore, the practice of detachment from family and friends is strictly imposed.

Brothers and sisters are always seated separately during meditation and meal times. My curiosity had become unstoppable. The code of conduct was unlike anything I had come across before. Admittedly the division between brothers and sisters at times felt arduous, as I preferred the company of men over women. Though this was all new and I was willing to discover the benefits.

I had to remind myself that the BK female community were not typical and after all we were practising soul consciousness, which was considered neither male nor female. Today I would question such rules, that virtually say, 'we do not trust you therefore you have to be kept apart so as not be tempted.'

Crazy I Followed Them All

I was intrigued and curious to discover where such disciplines would lead me. I took the BK disciplines very seriously, as it was made clear to me that one would not be allowed to attend meetings if the rules were not followed precisely. Since I was influenced and taught by Maryam, a close disciple of Dadi and also Dadi directly, I felt committed, and followed the disciplines with absolute dedication. Perhaps it was brainwashing tactics I was surrounded by, or the fact that I was excited by the newness of it all. I cannot explain it precisely but following the disciplines felt immensely seductive.

That is not to say that there were not some uncomfortable moments. I was observed and often told off for all sorts of things, such as for dressing too fashionably. I had designed my own modern version of the white uniform that I preferred wearing over the traditional white kurtas that most of the BK wore, I chose to ignore these corrections that were thrown at me. I was buzzing with excitement with all the new experiences I was gaining, and such instructions appeared unimportant to me. On another occasion, I was taken aside by a senior sister and told off for being too pretty. It was then explained to me that observing purity heightens one's attraction and I was reminded that I should avoid any form of contact with the brothers, which I barely had.

I could only describe such criticism as weird. I felt the critical eyes of the senior sister hovering over me, which I felt carried a sense of jealousy and bitterness. At times, these confrontations evoked a feeling of guilt as though I had done something wrong although my behaviour was innocent. I was in fact intrigued to discover the celibate lifestyle.

Did those teachers and sisters seriously question my trust? Thankfully, my own wisdom prevailed and I was able to overcome and ignore their judgments. I continued my practise, and my creativity clearly spiralled. There was no way I could stop creating. For some reason, my desires to create and learn were amplified because of my meditative practise. I was fascinated by what my mind was capable of, and the new heightened level of joy I discovered during mediation felt enticing. I was glowing and could feel the changed effect I had on the people around me. Over time, all of the disciplines became a habit, and would feel like the most natural thing to do. My senses kept heightened, I became very receptive to energy, plus my meditation moments became sharply tuned. There were moments I felt like a superhuman, as my practise became so intense. I found myself able to tap into other people's thoughts and emotions, as they stood in front of me or walked past me. I intuitively sensed their sufferings, troubles, and joys. With only five or six hours of sleep every night, I had to learn how to power nap for a few minutes. At times, I even found myself sleeping with my eyes open.

Although the teachings of the BK told me to deny my desires, instinctively I wanted to use the energy that was pulsing through me that I can only describe as passion. I felt highly inspired with all sorts of ideas about how I would like to express this new energy that was flowing through me. However, all my brilliant ideas were overruled by the doctrine which I had to observe thus denying my authenticity.

The Secret Gatherings

We were on our way to a place unlike anything I had ever experienced before. It took several months of preparation before I was officially allowed to visit the Brahma Kumaris World Spiritual University headquarters in Mount Abu, India, known as Madhuban. I had been given special permission by Dadi to visit Madhuban. A period of strict discipline and chastity, for a minimum of six months but usually up to a year, is required of the BK student before being allowed to stay in Madhuban. Madhuban translates as 'the Forest of Honey.' It is the headquarters of the BKWSU located on Mount Abu in the Aravalli mountain range of Rajasthan, India. This was my first visit to India and I still remember this journey as one of the most special experiences I had during my time as a BK. Madhuban on Mount Abu is the most picturesque and peaceful place I have ever visited. I was on my way to yet another spiritual adventure an encounter with 'Bapdada.'

Myself, Maryam and Adeline landed in Ahmedabad. A wonderful feeling of belonging wrapped around me on arrival. Ahmedabad was sunny and hot, it had a distinctive atmosphere incomparable to London, it felt as though I had landed into another dimension, India felt surreal yet mesmerising. For some reason, the heat did not have much of an effect on me. I sensed a pleasant breeze dancing around me as though the elements were adjusting themselves to provide me with the most comfortable experience possible.

We were picked up at the airport by a young BK sister in a white sari who welcomed us without words but instead, greeted us with a profound glimpse of *Drishti*, a smile, pink flower petals, and refreshments. Entranced by this divine welcome, we were chauffeured in a rattling minibus to the BK Ahmedabad centre which was close to the airport. The centre served as a stopover and was created specially to make the long journey to Mount Abu more comfortable. This was a place where BKs could eat, have a shower and meditate, before embarking on a further five hour car journey.

As our journey continued along the bumpy, dusty roads of India towards the slopes of Mount Abu, I spent my time dreaming about the intriguing stories I had heard about this mysterious land, it was legend that the Gods would retreat to this sacred mountain and immerse themselves in meditational solitude to gain their spiritual powers. As we arrived at the base of Mount Abu, I gazed out of the car window, we had reached the first campus of the spiritual headquarters complex. At the bottom of the mountain lay a massive white meditation hall. 'This is the place where Bapdada comes,' Maryam whispered to us. It was the busiest campus out of the three.

Madhuban consisted of three campuses, two more being located further up the mountain. Our drive continued on a winding road, up the slopes for a further thirty minutes moving into the tranquil seclusion of Mount Abu's lush vegetation and natural splendour. *'Many great sages, saints, and prophets from different religions achieved enlightenment in this powerful environment,'* our driver explained. At the end of the curvy road, nestled near the still waters of Nakki Lake, was Madhuban our journey was at an end, we had arrived at our sacred destination.

We stopped to greet Dadi Janki, and Dadi Gulzar, the heads of the organisation in their private quarters. As I stepped out of the car and looked around the campus it felt very special. I was induced by an alluring atmosphere and surrounded by a captivating energy. I was meeting Dadi Gulzar for the first time who like Dadi Janki had a commanding yet gentle presence with a distinctive personality. Dadi Gulzar was one of the original disciples of the founder. Her role at Madhuban was unique.

She became the exclusive corporeal medium of the consciousness known as 'Bapdada' the non-physical entity of the founder Brahma Baba who had died in 1969. This was the time when I first learned more about non-physical transmissions, having had an out of body experience myself I could easily relate to what I was presented with. The spirit of 'Bapdada' enters the body of Dadi Gulzar and takes complete control over her senses, vision, and speech in order to deliver messages to the BK leaders with instructions for the administration of the organisation. Those mysterious and unique meetings only happen in Madhuban at a particular time.

After taking Drishti from the two Dadis, we made our way to the newest campus, a few minutes' drive further up the mountain. We drove through a security gate into the estate surrounded by a white wall. A tastefully constructed campus with a lush green landscape laid in front of us. The quarters were energy efficient, electricity being generated by wind turbines and one of the largest solar panel installations in India.

This was to be our home for the next fourteen days. After settling into my room, I began to explore the grounds. Within the colourful plantation I discovered enchanting meditation huts of different shapes, some were domes and others were pyramids. These were mainly used for the 4:00am meditation, each providing a different meditation experience. There were plenty of buildings spread across the campus, study rooms and large halls which provided space for collective reflection. The campus was busy yet satisfyingly peaceful. Everyone kept strictly to their routines and contributing to this prevailing energy.

Madhuban was well organised with this special calm environment that allowed us to entirely focus on our spiritual progress. Everything was taken care of by the residents, sisters and brothers and some selected local people that helped to maintain the grounds. All our meals were prepared, and our rooms cleaned daily.

When large groups of BKs came together in the meditation halls for collective meditation the spike in energy was undeniable. The white uniforms and high hygiene standards that were followed served us very well in the hot climate. The meditation rooms always appeared fresh, no matter how many of us would be sitting together. Our body pores did not emit bad smells due to the purity of our diet and the multiple showers we took throughout the day, combined with the fresh mountain atmosphere. The discipline started to make sense and it made the simple surroundings particularly comfortable.

The Encounter

I was sitting cross legged on a concrete floor, padded with only a thin layer of white carpet in the giant meditation hall at the base of Mount Abu. Looking over my shoulder, I could see rows of neatly aligned Yogis sitting cross legged dressed in white gowns awaiting to witness this extraordinary event.

Thousands had arrived from all over the world to witness Bapdada speak through the body of Dadi Gulzar. Bapdada is recognised to be the essence of two souls Shiv Baba and Lekhraj Khubchand Kirpalani, also known as Dada Lekhraj the founder of the Brahma Kumaris. Born in 1876 in Hyderabad, in what is today Pakistan and passed away in 1969 in Mount Abu, India.

The hall with a capacity of 10,000 people, was filled with men and women from all walks of life, eagerly awaiting the entrance of the corporeal medium Dadi Gulzar. The bustling auditorium fell silent as Dadi Gulzar entered the hall and stepped on to the raised stage and took her place in the large armchair, an attendant brought a microphone and placed it in front of her. My focus was drawn towards her. Dadi Gulzar sat comfortably with a stillness projecting a natural sense of serenity into the huge space. Her powerful presence captivating everyone. The auditorium transformed in to an ocean of stillness. Everyone had joined the silent meditative call. My gaze was gently resting on Dadi Gulzar's forehead, as she sat, ready for the non-physical entity of Bapdada to take over her body. The entrancing energy in this enclosed environment made it easy to completely withdraw from the rest of the world.

Then there was the moment, Gulzar's body jerked, and the transformation became apparent, the consciousness of Bapdada took over and Bapdada began to address everyone with his gaze. I had never witnessed an atmosphere so highly charged, I felt wrapped in an energy ball of bliss and contentment. He then slowly began to speak into the microphone. Dadi Gulzar's voice had transformed to a deep, elongated soft whisper with a profound, wise and authoritative tone. At the same time, I witnessed an altered expression on Dadi's face.

Dadi Gulzar's facial expressions transformed becoming more masculine yet captivatingly beautiful. The words that echoed through the speakers felt as if they were spoken just for me, although others felt the same way. The atmosphere felt lusciously intoxicating, nothing really mattered anymore, as the words floated through the air I plunged into a blissful state of invigorated love, which needed no explanation. The transmission lasted over four hours, I had no explanation for what I was witnessing, or how I managed to sit cross legged for so long on a hard concrete floor only covered by a thin carpet.

My stay in Madhuban was turning into a spiritual adventure. The following ten days were divine, I floated in and out of classes during the day and woke early with great ease, eager to begin my practise in one of the pyramid shaped meditation huts. In Madhuban, everything was different to the London branch. There was no one correcting or trying to fix me, as everyone seemed to be preoccupied with their own newfound bliss and effortless practises.

After this experience, I returned to Madhuban yearly, eager to reengage with its beauty and wonder. There is no clear point or real official recognition of celebrating a BK status within the organisation it arises through personal recognition. Dadi Janki symbolically honoured my bond to Shiv Baba (God) with a gift. On my first visit to Madhuban I received a silver ring, a year later a gold ring, and a gold necklace the year after. The rings symbolised my matrimony to Shiv Baba.

Our World's Energy Grid Points

When I began to distance myself from the BK, I missed the atmosphere of Mount Abu the most, I longed to be back amongst the mountains. What was this energy I had experienced? At the time, I believed it was unique to Mount Abu. Later, I learned that this energy can be found in many places around the world. Like the human energy field our planet also has universal energy points that are connected to an energy grid around the Earth, which peaks in various sites on each continent.

The measurable global electromagnetic Schumann resonances known as Ley lines are powerful energy strands carrying Earth's magnetic field that runs like a grid across the surface of the planet. Imagine the grid like the pattern of a crystal snowflake. Energy is carried along the lines and where the energy lines cross are highly concentrated magnetic points of spiralling energy, also referred to as vortex access points. These higher vibrational intersecting points are understood to work like vibrational transmitters, carrying information or energy to be distributed around the planet. All Ley lines connect to this planetary grid through vortexes which sustain all life. Just like our solar system is a spiralling vortex with the planets spinning around the Sun. Also the same is the smallest atom spiralling in a vortex like a miniature solar system, wheels within wheels within wheels.

Some of our magnificent wildlife navigates by the Earth's magnetic field, utilising those energy strands like a compass. Such as migrating birds like swallows route their way to warmer climates during winter months and fish such as salmon and sharks and mammals like whales and dolphins and reptiles like marine turtles use the magnetic field to navigate the planet sometimes travelling thousands of miles to the exact location of their breeding grounds. Researchers have discovered that even insects such as bees navigate using the Earth's magnetic field.

More wondrous is that Ley lines are also flowing in line with underground streams and magnetic currents. The most extraordinary part is that the Earth's

Ley lines draw straight lines throughout the world aligning prominent landmarks such as the Pyramids. Secret and mystical structures such as megaliths, churches, temples, stone circles, holy wells, and burial sites are also found to be built on Ley line portals. I discovered that Madhuban was one of them.

We are naturally attracted to those locations recognising them as places of peacefulness, and we resonate with the energy they project. They assist our growth and evolution, we can retreat to these places to seek alignment and peace. There are significant energy vortexes with thousands of smaller ones spread all over the planet, they are never too far away. They can be open spaces, such as woodland or mountains, they are also present in dense cities. Some are more famous than others, for example, In England we have Glastonbury, Stonehenge, Shaftesbury and the coast of Cornwall. Around the world are many known energy points such as Sedona in Arizona and Mount Shasta in California, Easter Island in Polynesia, Lake Titicaca and Machu Picchu in Peru, the Great Pyramid of Giza and Mount Sinai in Egypt, the Mount of Olives in Jerusalem, Mount Kailash in the Himalayas Tibet, Kauai in Hawaii, Mount Etna in Sicily, and many more.

Closer to my home I also found that London has many small points of energy sites, Primrose Hill and Hampstead Heath are wonderful spots to recharge. These energy points provide possibilities for us to align and expand and are beautiful places for meditation. The intrinsic nature of these energy grids is to magnify the energy correlated to our body that lies as the basis of our physical reality. Merging with these vibrations can supercharge us and are most beneficial when we seek upliftment. When I meditate at such points the experience is unique, I often receive frequencies like downloads which are focused directly at me. One can have the most exhilarating connective experience at such places or the most painful ones as we let go of old hurts. Whatever energy one brings to those energy points will be amplified. Those points can be catalysts for healing, when pains are amplified it provides us with an opportunity to face them, address them, and ask for assistance to release them. Ultimately to be freed.

Sometimes I am drawn randomly to enter local churches whilst travelling. I never attend services but prefer to sit in a state of appreciation and observe the energy those structures draw in, some feel innocent and peaceful whilst with others I sense powerful polarities which I prefer to stay away from.

We all have heard of or may have seen spooky shrine like structures, known to be used for rituals, such as animal, human or child sacrifices. I pondered what could possibly be the purpose of any such rituals performed at sacred sites which have been depicted in historical scriptures, books, or even present day stories of a satanic Hollywood and secret societies.

Vortex intersectional points are often used to tamper with the energy grid of earth to dim human consciousness, focused on specific areas, through rituals, or with artificial satellite holograms that override the Earth's natural grid. It is nothing new that our reality is being simulated and projected by some form of technology outside of our physical reality. One can read about many interesting findings shared by researchers about the mechanisms of advanced technology and how our perception resonates and interacts with the energy of the world around us. Churches act as amplifying points. I often wondered why churches and cathedrals were built with so many pointed spikes. The reason for those pointed towers is that they function like antennas to increase the communication with other planes to assist, tune and connect to divine guidance. The same applies to crowns hence kings would wear crowns with crystal and quartzes that serve as amplifiers. Myth has it that kings would sometimes tune into undivine planes, causing an undivine ruling.

While all those beautiful places have their purpose. I learnt to never underestimate our own energy field, that can be created around one's own body. Our own energy field can move us through dimensions, no matter where we are on the globe. We can form our own high frequency vortex that travels with us wherever we go.

Follow Your Dreams

It was 4.00am I felt sleepy, but I would never miss attending the early morning meditation which we referred to as "Amritvela" translated it means "time of nectar." We were taught and understood this to be the purest time of the day, prior to dawn, when most people are still asleep, there is less 'thought traffic' in the surrounding field, therefore facilitating the meditative experience when tuning in to divine powers and knowledge. At this time when stillness prevails, I had entered the meditation room at the Brahma Kumaris retreat, set in the parklands of Nuneham Courtenay in Oxfordshire, England, where I was staying to partake in and help facilitate a spiritual retreat. I had started to question my life having been a BK for almost five years and felt I was not making much progress, things had started to feel the same and I was seeking newness, clarity and most of all stability.

I joined the silent meditation room that was filled with my fellow Yogi sisters and brothers who had gathered for our early morning Amritvela routine. I admired the grand hall of this noble manor house, which had once been occupied by English aristocracy. Located in the middle of the countryside, with the river Thames winding past the grounds, the name of the manor was Nuneham House, well known for its picturesque grounds. Owned by Oxford University and used by the Brahma Kumaris World Spiritual University as their Global Retreat Centre. The meditation room was a splendid open space with high ceilings and elegant floor to ceiling windows.

The grand space was filled with over forty people. I took my place in one of the large padded white chairs, wrapped myself in my soft white meditation shawl and began to focus, by gently resting my eyes half open on the point of light that was drawn onto the large painting in front of me. A soft soothing melody was filling the room, as I was gently drawn into the canvas, I sensed the light rays of the painting expanding projecting into the room wrapping around me, I felt safely concealed into a sea of white and golden light, the contentment

I had longed for, the reality of the room had faded away, a soothing whisper of words started flooded into my mind…

'Do not worry, my treasured one…everything is temporary, nothing ever stays the same…every moment is a new moment… You are experiencing the feelings of sameness only because you are observing in the same fashion…you are the creator of all your experience…make it your mission to feel your best moment by moment…you are loved…'

As the whisper in my mind was fading into the distance, I felt the adoration those words were spoken with, I wanted desperately to hold onto this sensation, it had felt so wise and comforting. The more I tried to hold on, the further away the feeling faded, as my awareness transferred back into the room I observed how everything around me was made from light, the molecules were vibrating speedily to create solid objects, as I was sensing the solidness, my consciousness shifted fully and I found myself back in the solid environment of the room I had entered. I looked around and found myself sitting alone, everyone had left. I had lost all sense of time and awareness, the thirty minute meditation session had finished.

Who had spoken to me? The message I had received was contrary to the teaching of the BK. I had loyally followed the instructions of the Brahma Kumaris but had recently developed doubts and now I began to further question the doctrine I had been following.

The Fragrance of Mumbai

It was 2003, I was thirty-two years old and had begun teaching meditation. I was running classes in various Yoga centres in London, as a result I felt inspired to design a clothing collection based on my spiritual studies which I named 'Il Rosario', in English the Rosary. The collection would be designed specifically for meditation. I had discussed my ideas with brother Bonthi, a businessman who also frequented the BK's headquarters. We agreed to develop the idea into samples in his factory in Mumbai India. Brother Bonthi was a frequent traveller to Mumbai and was also close to the BK family based in Mumbai.

I joined one of his trips and landed in the vibrant city of Mumbai. I had returned to India this time for a different experience. This was my first visit to Mumbai, I was excited to discover a new part of India. As I stepped out of the aircraft into the daylight, I inhaled the air of Mumbai, the warm and humid salty aroma of the ocean mixed with traffic fumes, fried palm oil and the fragrance of incense. Having passed through passport control I was soon chauffeured to the apartment provided for my stay in the centre of the city.

After freshening up I was picked up by brother Bonthi, as I had agreed to join him to meet the sisters at the BK centre in Kandivali, a neighbourhood in the north of Mumbai which was an area mostly secluded from tourism. Our local driver skilfully navigated us through the streets of Mumbai heading to our destination. We drove through the vibrant streets teeming with life and on traffic packed highways and down narrow dusty roads.

The theatre of life that played out in front of me was unlike anything I had seen before. I watched a chorus of cars appear randomly from different directions with their horns blasting, it seemed that traffic lights were just there for decoration. The echoes of rumbling lorries and the buzzing of auto rickshaws were relentless. The highroads were also well travelled by wandering cows, bicycles and pedestrians as well as littered with all types of debris. What I can only describe as either madness or organised chaos left me astounded as to how everyone arrived at their destination in one piece. As we were chauffeured safely by our expert Indian driver to our destination, I became convinced that every day a God given intervention must be at hand on the roads of India.

Whilst the car journey to Kandivali was an adventure on its own, the enchanted encounter that awaited me was yet another sweet surprise. At a short distance away from the chaotic highways, the fumes of the traffic had subsided and the scent in the air had turned into a mix of aromas of cinnamon, cardamom and clove from the burning *agarbattis*.

We reached the front door of the first floor flat where we were greeted with a big welcome by three beautiful BK sisters who were curiously waiting, dressed in white sarees, the uniform of the Brahma Kumaris and each wearing their status badge. These three young women oversaw the running of the BK Kandivali centre. Surekha, Dipti and Ila. The senior sister in charge was Surekha. The sister's ages ranged from early twenties to early thirties. All three welcomed me with much excitement, an instant bond was formed, it felt like I had just met my long lost sisters. Their curiosity was most charming, they wanted to know all about my journey, I was intrigued by their benevolence. When they learned that I was sleeping alone in an apartment, they insisted that I should stay with them, they found it unimaginable that I could possibly consider sleeping alone. Their apartment consisted of a fairly large living room, a kitchen, two bedrooms and a bathroom. All three sisters lived there and it was also used as the main BK centre for meditation in this part of Mumbai, serving their local community by providing a space for spiritual practice, comfort, and hope.

Every inch of the apartment had been utilised the living room was used as the main lecture room for the daily morning classes and turned into a dining room for meal times. A second room was the silent room that we would call Baba's room, a room for meditation that turned into a bedroom at night. Then there was the master bedroom, which was used to store their personal belongings and was a permanent bedroom. *'But where would I sleep?'* I asked. Surekha explained, *'Dipti and Ila will share Baba's room to sleep, and we will share the main bedroom,'* which was expressed as the most natural thing to do, and indeed to them it was. My concern at making them uncomfortable was an unaccepted argument. I was asked to collect my belongings and join them at the centre. I was pleased they had convinced me, I felt very pleased and excited that I would be able to stay with them.

So my next spiritual adventure began in the bustling city of Mumbai. I never saw much sun whilst in Mumbai, the city woke up to hazy skies most days due to the heavy pollution. Mumbai was hot and dusty, but my days were busy and filled with so much newness that none of that affected me. Living among traditions that were out of my comfort zone took my undivided attention, I had to adjust to this exciting experience of new routines. Every night before going to sleep we would tuck in each other's mosquito nets that hung over our beds to protect us from bites, we had no modern mosquito spray or repellents only traditional incense. The sisters explained that if we keep our meditation practice high and united with Baba's light, the mosquitos would not bite, the mosquito net was there for additional prevention, but our practice kept us safe, it seemed to work as none of us were bitten not even once.

All three sisters were uniquely beautiful, radiant, and wise each with distinctive characteristics. Sister Surekha was authoritative, yet gentle, she was slender and tall with the physique of an empress, she had to endure a lot of pain due to an illness. Dipti was smart focused and hard working. Ila was pretty, with a wonderful sense of humour that kept us amused all day long. Sister Surekha suffered from a rare muscular illness that stiffened her body during sleep. Every morning and evening, two or three mothers would come to the centre to jointly massage Surekha's muscles to ease her pain. These mothers were married and lived with their families, and were part of the local community that supported each other and had developed their own systems to aid healing amongst themselves.

The centre was constantly busy with people coming and going all day. Surekha and I slept in a large bed but before sleeping we would massage each other's faces and share stories. We would amuse ourselves by talking about some of the strange and alien lifestyle patterns in the Western world. Surekha's chosen purpose was to become a mother and wife and marry in a white wedding dress. I felt amused that this European tradition had taken to her liking. Surekha knew that her current celibate status was a transitional lifestyle. Surekha had been a part of the BKs since childhood and had grown up in the BK environment. In India, it was not unusual for young women to live a committed spiritual life until they decide to marry. This surprised me as it was most unlike the strict doctrine I had to obey in the London BK centre, where thoughts like that would be judged against doctrine and discouraged. Surekha was free and unhindered by her desires, there was no trace of guilt, but instead conviction. How admirable I thought.

Every morning we awoke early at 3.30am, showered, attended our Amritvela meditation practice, and prepared for the 6.30am class when people from the neighbourhood would come and gather for the daily spiritual lectures. It was a bustling centre, although we all sat on the floor there was never enough space for everyone. Every morning Surekha read out the Murli in Hindi to everyone while I read the English version to myself, the Murli are the collected teachings from Bapdada that are channelled via Dadi Gulzar. The class concluded with the soothing sounds of a Hindi melody that prompted everyone to meditate. On some occasions I conducted the meditation. One morning I sat in front of the group with my gaze resting on the people that had gathered, we were exchanging profound Drishti. I could sense the hardship many of those people have had to endure, most of them were very simply dressed, yet I felt how precious and unique each one of them was. I saw their soul's light shining, each one had a role that was so valuable and important to the existence of this planet, it became so apparent how unique each one was, *'Though why did they not know how special they are?'* I asked silently. In the screen of my mind, I was shown a veil that laid over them, their memories dormant to knowing their own greatness. I asked, *'Though how is this possible. Who put this veil there?'* I heard in reply the whisper of a soft voice, *'Do you see they are yet to awaken to their own greatness.'*

'Am I dormant too?' I asked. At this point, the meditation music stopped, concluding the session.

It was time to distribute Toli which is a home-made sweet that is traditionally handed to everyone that takes Drishti. A queue formed in front of me everyone lined up to take Toli and Drishti. As I passed the Toli individually I gazed into those human eyes, mesmerised by their marvellous light reflecting right back at me. It was unusual for the locals to see a Western face in their Kandivali centre, especially conducting meditation, this encounter was unique, although more for myself than for them.

The days that followed remained somehow enchanted, I had adopted a completely new lifestyle and assisted with the service in the morning, evening, and weekends, during the day I would be at the factories to complete my assignment. In the early evening I returned to the centre. Many young mothers with happy children visited us, large dinners would be prepared and we would eat together. I tasted their local homemade Indian cuisine which was highly spiced with the most potent chilli peppers, in fact it was so hot that it was uneatable, tears ran down my cheeks like a waterfall. Mumbai's traditional Indian food is always heavily spiced. Even the mildest version separately prepared for me was still impossible for me to consume. Everyone was bewildered by my sensitivity to their spices. They told me that to them the food they had prepared separately for me tasted totally bland.

On the weekends we attended the larger spiritual gatherings at the nearby centres to meet the senior Didi's. The Kandivali centre had a duty to report their process to the senior Didi's. For those meetings it was compulsory that the uniforms were worn, the white saree with their status badge. The saree is an elegant garment worn by BK sisters which is draped in a unique way around the body. White had been chosen by the founder as the symbol of purity. In India sarees are usually reserved for special occasions but it is the everyday uniform for all BK sisters. We were required to present ourselves neatly and uniformly.

Whilst I was always wearing white, I had opted for the Kurta when on duty which consists of a long white blouse and loose pants instead of the official uniform. For practicality it was not expected of the UK sisters to wear sarees. Although For this occasion I was to wear the traditional saree. I had to be shown how to drape, walk and sit in this traditional Indian attire. Secretly I was looking forward to wearing a saree I had not worn one before. Well, my dressing up turned into a lively event. All my three sisters were masters of this trade, showing me simultaneously how to drape this complex dressage over my body, with some pulling and twisting and mirth the fabric was finally gracefully laying over my body. I truly felt appreciation for the magnificent diversity of our cultures, allowing me to explore so much further, connecting me with India's hospitality and benevolence.

After our morning meeting our weekend outings would continue to Mumbai's beaches. A small group of us, sisters and brothers would join together for an afternoon picnic. Taking us away from any duties and unbothered by the unfortunately polluted beach, we playfully strolled bare foot along the sandy beaches hand in hand, in our white sarees simply thrilled by our company. Everything was so different in the Kandivali BK centre. This centre seemed to be beaming with love. I started to question the UK's BK centres where I was observed and instructed to obey the very strict doctrine that overruled love, closeness and kindness.

I ended up living with my sisters at the Kandivali BK centre for four weeks. There I was in Mumbai sharing a small, simple yet unique space, in a city that was covered in dust, far away from the comfort of the Western world and my pretty Kensington apartment in London. Yet I had lived surrounded by love that had exceeded all the luxury I had been accustomed to.

To end this chapter by coming fast forwards to the present day, Sister Surekha's dream was realised, she bonded with a brother who had been instrumental in ensuring Surekha was receiving the right medical support and bringing about an improvement in her health. They fell in love and ended up marrying. Today Surekha is the mother of a wonderful boy.

Spiritual Discipline Not Enough

Being a celibate Yogini BK sister, I had undeniably mesmerising moments mainly in the first five years. I met the BK when I was twenty eight years old. This new adventure felt surreal and was a catalyst to expanding my consciousness, yet it also had disadvantages. The teachings of the Brahma Kumaris imposed many rules to prepare for a life in a golden age and a paradise on a future Earth, but it was not clear when this was supposed to happen. We were often labelled by outsiders as being brainwashed, we even had our own private jokes about it. Our brains were indeed washed and supposedly freed from negative influences and vices. In reality, I had my brain washed with rules and restrictive beliefs instilled by a strict discipline. I would listen to the ideology of the BK during a state of mind when I was at my most receptive to these influences which was in the early hours of morning.

Yet still my personal connection with my higher being persisted with clarity brought through my meditation which little by little revealed the misguided doctrine I had been taught. Suddenly the BK doctrine was not valid anymore, and I started to question things. Somehow years had flown by and though my life had seemed exciting at times, besides my adventures with the BK, another part of my life had not quite worked out. I had many extraordinary experiences and discovered many things that most people do not know exist. However, there was still so much I desired to be, attain, and explore. I found myself at a point where I knew the life of a celibate and disciplined Brahma Kumaris Yogi sister was over for me I could no longer justify adhering to what I now realised was an illogical doctrine. I wondered how seven long years of dedication had passed so fast, during my altered state of mind I had almost lost all sense of time or age.

Baby Steps

It was a moment of hopelessness. I felt like crying, '*Angels do not cry,*' Dadi Janki had once said as I streamed with tears in front of her. She handed me her personal cotton handkerchief to dry my tears. I remember thinking very few people carry cotton handkerchiefs around these days. I would usually go to see Dadi to update her with my progress, however I had gone to her for advice instead. There was little progress in my spiritual development to talk about and my whole life felt like it was in a turmoil. I did not know which direction to go, I felt in conflict with the rules I had to obey about my life's purpose, rather than following my own intuition. I felt anything but an angel and it was not really what I wanted to become either. I had let go of my dreams and ambitions and felt like a failure as much as I loved my spiritual evolution, I could not understand why I had to limit myself to be one or the other.

Why could I not just be who I desired to be and combine my spiritual wisdom with my ambitions? This I believed was what living life to its fullest potential meant. All the limitations imposed on me felt suddenly wrong. I had spent over seven years of my life in the service of others while they benefited, I felt restricted, and my ambitions were a world apart from my current surroundings. I was still dreaming of pursuing my own independent business. To add to my confusion, the signals I received through my meditation kept guiding me to follow my aspirations and thus contradicted the BK rules. I was considered a surrender BK sister, therefore as per Maryam's instructions, I was to seek advice from Dadi Janki, I was not to take actions without consulting the seniors. I remembered my last meeting with Dadi clearly, as instructed I had gone to her for advice. Dadi's energy felt comforting, and my tears were coming slowly to an end. Although the advice Dadi had offered, to move to the retreat centre in Oxfordshire and become a resident was the last thing I wanted to hear. I felt even more trapped by the thought of it. '*Dadi, but this is not what I want to do,*' I expressed those words with anguish. Dadi looked at me and spoke, '*Then follow what you must do but ensure you keep close to Dadi and write every week to update her with your progress.'* I felt relieved to be liberated, the guilt I had about following my own chosen path was dissolving, and I handed back her handkerchief. *'Keep that handkerchief, it will dry all your tears,'* I heard Dadi say. Months after our last meeting, I pulled out Dadi's handkerchief and remembered her words. I had distanced myself from Dadi and had not kept in touch as she had suggested. Sometimes I felt regret and thought I should write to her. However, I never followed through. The thought of falling back to let someone continue to rule me felt wrong.

I still attended classes from time to time at the BK London headquarters, detaching myself had not been easy as I was embracing newness there were still aspects, I missed from my BK life. However, I was determined to create a new experience without compromises. In a moment of weakness, I felt tearful, I found myself holding Dadi's handkerchief. I noticed that it was handcrafted, very likely by one of the local sisters in India. It had colourful floral embroidery around its corners. By admiring the craftsmanship of the handkerchief, I tried to distract myself from my worrisome thoughts. Captivated by the intriguing design I fell into a trance like state, it seemed as if the handkerchief had some sort of magic to it. I gently dabbed the handkerchief to dry my tears, whilst feeling a soothing tingling on my face as though the fabric was caressing my cheeks, like gently stroking hands. Gazing at the handkerchief, I wondered what it was that had felt so gentle. I lingered over the embroidered flowers and petals and saw that the vibrant flowers were absorbing my tears. I saw pinks, yellows, and greens and a gentle breeze started to softly sway the petals, as if by a magic spell. A comforting aroma of sweet blossoms floated around me, I felt calm, then the flowers on the handkerchief spoke to me.

'Hold your aspirations firmly in your mind and become one with them, then all will be forthcoming. Become the vibrational counterpart of your desires. Universal energies that are beyond your human comprehension are ready for you to facilitate the delivery. Allow your vibrational alignment, and you will witness the magic of your own creative power. Circumstances and people will present themselves to you, watch it all unfold in front of your eyes, you will be amazed when you discover your own creative powers.'

During my BK life, I was taught to renounce all my creative interests and aspirations. Many religious establishments teach these beliefs, that renouncing everything is a noble way of living. Since I had denied my desires and did not aspire to much, I could not help but notice that the advice I had been given was satisfying to others, but it did not serve me well. I had put my dreams on hold and hit rock bottom. My finances were tumbling, and I found myself in a situation where I had never been before. I felt vulnerable. I had always considered myself a stable person and capable of finding my way through life. I could not help but reflect on the life and ambition I once had. I had shut down my dreams and labelled them as unimportant and had followed the dictates of others. I felt deceived by my spiritual studies and started to dislike my situation. I was desperately asking for new knowledge, a way that would lead me out of this unsatisfactory situation. I had misunderstood the importance of desires and had put my worthiness at stake. There was so much more to learn and experience. I wanted to go out into the world and start again.

Having been obedient to regulations and doctrine during my BK life, I was now determined to be free from any rules. I wanted to break away from any restriction that my BK life had imposed upon me. I wanted freedom from anything that was hindering my expansion or authenticity so I could live to my fullest potential. With all my boldness, I began doing only the things I wanted to do. I broke my routine and attended meditation classes on my own terms only when I felt like it and slept when I desired to. There were of course, those moments when I felt overcome by conflicting emotions and guilt. Yet I was determined and worked through them I chose to acknowledge my guilt and identified it as a sentiment which did not get me anywhere since I was done with undervaluing myself, guilt had to be overridden by self-love.

As I eased into my newfound freedom, it did not take me long to realise how hard I had been on myself. I was confirming self-love daily and started to feel confident about my decision to break free from the bondage of being ruled over by someone else's ideology. I was on the road to embracing the world through my spiritual mind as well as my physical senses. I decided to become fully expressive with my physical body in a way I have never been before. I was ready to come back to a new me and I was ready to break all the rules I had been trained to obey.

The End of Chastity

Alexander had been a BK brother for over fifteen years, he was handsome with sparkling eyes and a luminous face. I had known Alexander since the very start, he was more relaxed than most of the other BKs. With a successful career, he had travelled the world and had created some star status within the BK. We had brief meetings at the BK centre but years later our paths collided, I found a new friend who joined my sporty activities, something that had not been encouraged in our BK world. We would hang out, jog, or skate the streets of London. Spending more time away from the BK environment brought to light how spellbound I had been under the BK's strict regimes. I started to lose interest in attending my spiritual classes as I learned about a side of the BK world I had not known existed. I had always believed that every BK brother and sister were as dedicated to their disciplines as I and Maryam. I came to realise that this was not the case, there were strictures kept on the sisters but the brothers seemed to be less controlled. Also like every religious organisation there were the scandals, the BK had them too and the secret stories started to emerge all around me. I was told about secret affairs, where celibacy was broken, and love affairs kindled between senior sisters and brothers. I learned of a tragic suicide of a sister who was overcome by guilt for having broken her celibacy. I also learned of thefts, money scandals and even murder in India. It transpired that these stories had been circulating around the clan for years. Everyone seemed to know about them. But the baffling thing was that I had never heard anything in my seven years as a BK sister. It was as though the protective magic bubble around the BK had popped. My sacred place, my field of pure, innocent space had been a creation of my altered mind.

Months passed and Alexander kept joining me in spontaneous little adventures, our casual encounters had declared themselves as desirable, I determinedly was breaking every rule in the book. With curiosity, and armed with a charmed authenticity our friendship led to our first touch, as our skin brushed on one another, our eyes met and our lips merged, then suddenly we were lovers. As our bodies glided into one another, our sexual senses blended into a perfectly orchestrated union. Conventional orgasm as I remembered was not conventional anymore. At the climax of our most intimate point, I felt an energy rising unlike any other resembling a divine spark ornamenting my female sensuality and new found freedom, leaving me mesmerised, sweetly satisfied and empowered. I felt a liquid running down my thighs, creating a large wet patch on our love bed. An orgasm but different. I had a female ejaculation. At the time I was unaware of the existence of female ejaculation, over the next weeks and months, my nonconformity escalated into pure enjoyment.

My spiritual practice had escalated my senses up to an unknown new level. My explicit decision to break my celibacy had opened an untouched state that flourished. I learned later that divinely the female ejaculation was thought of as sacred and rare.

Alexander and I were owning our encounters. Neither of us was particularly interested in an enduring commitment. Our connection was as good as it could get and that was all that mattered at that time. As our aspirations expanded in different directions, our bond faded, my seven years of celibacy had been broken, I had wanted something to happen and it did. I was satisfied with all that I had experienced.

I skipped all my spiritual evening classes and found other things to do. I joined the performing arts, dance and singing classes. My focused training had moulded me. I noticed an enhanced sensitivity to vibrational frequencies as I started to interact with other people. The disciplines I had followed kept me in a sheltered environment for years. As a BK, I had always surround myself with likeminded Yogis. I had now to relearn how to live with non BK people, and become accustomed to outside bodily contact again, even something as simple as a handshake. I would smell and hear vibrational sounds that most people could not sense, meat eaters carried a discomforting odour. I could detect the vibration of a smoker or drinker from a distance, excessive small talk, gossip and sounds that were out of harmony felt uncomfortable. At first, I did not understand how I had become so sensitive. Odour and sounds are vibrations that are translated by the body's senses, my cellular bodily senses had amplified, because of my mediative practice. Now energy was hitting my heightened senses in an entirely new way.

I felt terribly uncomfortable at my first dance class when I had to embrace my dance partner, I was picking up melanges of dense energy fractions from my dance partners. In time, I learned to adjust my auric field to shield me from any undesired frequencies, and dancing became one of my most exciting passions. I would dance for hours almost daily. I would spend every free minute on my new found enjoyments.

It was several months before I dared to take off the gold ring which had symbolically branded me a BK. Almost one year later, I finally let go of the necklace, it took me nearly two years to break away from the most basic of BK disciplines.

The Kiss

I was asked many times after leaving the BK life, if I had missed having sex during my years of celibacy. The truth is it rarely crossed my mind, when my attention was drawn to it I felt no reason to engage in it. Being celibate in that altered state of mind was an empowering way of being. All my energy was focused on the excitement of my spiritual expansion which felt immensely satisfying.

During my celibacy I recall once observing a couple kissing in public, I perceived it as a strange action. I felt glad I did not have to do that kind of thing. I viewed it from a different state of mind. I had kissed before, but at this moment it felt odd, one could compare it with a childlike observation. I also recall one very vivid dream I had around the same time.

I stood captured by a profound sensation of adoration, by a male spherical being that was focused solely on me, projecting undeniable adoration for me, I had been divinely kissed, an energetic exchange of the most profound sincerity. The most magical kiss which was intangible yet fully manifested within my emotions. It was beyond the normal physical or sensual experience I had ever known. When I awoke, this experience had penetrated every cell of my body. I did not see the face or body of whom I had merged with, instead I felt the presence of this authentic deep union the purity of love was unquestionable. I could still feel the enduring effects of the dream present in my body days after. This divine kiss had set a particular standard and catapulted my level of sensuality up to a completely new level.

Celibacy

'There is something very delicious and new when I do things which I have been absent from for a very long time.'

All our senses are geared up to be sensual, our eyes, ears, nose, tongue, skin are all sensors of sensuality everything about us is sensual, I am a sensual being for the enhancement of my physical experience. I grew up surrounded by a Sicilian Roman Catholic family where the sexual act outside of marriage was viewed as shameful yet I was born and raised in Germany where sexuality was not taboo. Sex was considered an enjoyable activity between two consenting individuals. In Germany, brothels are are legal. Instead of learning the traditional conservative attitude towards sex, German schools educated us about contraceptive practices and safe sex techniques thus indirectly endorsing casual sex. I was a product of both influences.

I had transitioned into a celibate lifestyle by the age of thirty and remained celibate for seven years. Paradoxically, having been celibate made me dig deeper into myself I also searched out various philosophies that led me to a greater understanding of what love making truly is. It was none of the things I had observed in romantic movies or novels. Nor was it to be found in my religious teaching. My experience with celibacy was unique, becoming and being celibate was as exciting as breaking it, there was a unique mystery that felt new and exciting on both occasions. I learned to understand so much about celibacy by experiencing it, celibacy did not determine the powers of my spiritual evolution. Being sensual is not being impure, it is senseless to consider oneself impure for this reason, thoughts of impurity only emerged when I dimmed my natural forces with impure beliefs about myself.

My spiritual development continued to deepen even after I broke my celibacy. Mental strength comes from focusing energy, sensual energy or creative energy are equal. Energy is energy, whether I apply it during love making, spiritually, building an empire or landscaping my garden.

I discovered that celibacy is understood by very few. How and if it is suitable is according to the individual. I was very curious about it although I am not for it or against it. Celibacy is a bespoke matter which is not only practised by certain faiths but high performance achievers such as sportsmen and athletes are also known to observe periods of abstinence to aid their focus and improve their ability.

The Sexual Link

Lovemaking and its climatic conclusion the orgasm have been devalued as porn, and lust, confederated with drugs and alcohol to disperse the real powers of this divine interaction. Alcohol plunges the human consciousness into a low frequency field. The sexual practice of pain and bondage whilst being drunk or drugged, stoops those who entertain themselves with it, inviting lower forces to linger around that feed upon such energies, always wanting more. Sensual experience will be minimal, and lust will increase thus sustaining a shallow loop of dependency, the result is sexual addiction.

There is a divine purpose to the unity a climax represents. Yet humanity has been brainwashed with sexual guilt to suppress natural sensuality. Endeavouring to deprive us of our self-empowerment, mass media has brainwashed us into guilt and shame and distorted our thinking and our sensualities. Instead of appreciating our magnificent bodies we are encouraged to be ashamed of them. Our bodies are works of art, capable of marvellous things, yet we have been trained to believe in our inadequacy and vulnerability. Our exceptional bodily senses are designed to tap into higher evolved frequencies, lovemaking raises our vibrational tone with the potential to tune us into a higher plane beyond this third dimensional reality. Only few comprehend the magnificence of lovemaking, those that understand the power of sexual energy will refrain from casual sex. Lovemaking is a pure super powerful exchange of two bonding partners. When this deeply sensual energy is exchanged with purity the intensity of this unique bond ripples through the universe and heals the world around us.

When couples love each other, they are bonded, and an energy circuitry opens that carries a higher frequency between them. This is not to cleave to one another forever but to honour each other's energy flow for however long it may last. The electrical current is raised higher because of the open circuitry that occurs through the bonding. There are even greater heights of orgasmic experience as the nervous system becomes able to handle the compatible frequencies that are received. A joint sexual climax is an amplifier that projects energy strands through our bodies that act like tuning forks and align us to a higher realm. Hence such orgasmic experience brings about a healing and realignment of the physical body. Imagine invoking such powerful frequencies which uplift everything in the atmosphere of the lover's field. If the partners do not love each other that circuitry will not open. They may still experience good sex, but the energy circuit will not flow to the higher level. One is not able to get close with someone who is not operating at the same frequency and will not be able to merge vibrationally. The dissonance causes discomfort and stress because of the need to continuously adapt to each other's vibration when involved intimately. All energy would be spent creating an adaptive mechanism. If one has a poorly evolved nervous system, the sexual experience will be very limited because the nervous system conducts the electrical current. If one entertains a secret sex life or a dysfunctional relationship and must manipulate energy to have sex, it will jeopardise one's integrity, such activities vibrate at the lower end of the spectrum. We have only ourselves to be responsible for raising our standards and with it our conscious awareness and by doing so we will discover the gourmet version of sexual energy.

My Karma?

There was a time when I believed I was doomed for life. I had no idea where I was going wrong. I did things according to the book. But why on Earth were things not working out for me? What was I doing wrong? How much harder did I need to work? 'It must be your Karma from a past life,' I was told. Since no one had been able to provide me with a better explanation, that was what I believed and felt, I was doomed for life. Though something inside me started doubting this idea. 'What karma?' I asked, I wondered surely there must be a way to fix it? Karma, as I was taught to believe, is one of the most misinterpreted ideas man has concocted about God, just like the theory of being sent to Hell. If God is supposed to be loving, kind and forgiving why would he be in judgement of me or anyone, evaluating my life to condemn me at my death to Hell, or back to Earth so that I can repeat life? To find my way out of dangerous situations and suffer for some misdemeanour I was supposed to have committed in a previous life in a completely different body, I don't remember. There was little logic to it, this was not something I could consider as the truth, our life is not about that. Why would God who is celebrated as all loving, judge me and command me to redeem myself? God could not possibly be part of any harmful act or thought, this would not be love. A true God represents pure, constant, stable, positive energy the ideology of Karma seemed primitive to me. As a BK, I was taught to believe in positive Karma that arises from being soul conscious and negative Karma that is motivated by body consciousness through our senses. Plainly speaking, according to BK doctrine the feelings I experience through my body are sinful. This, of course, must be untrue. This belief promotes the ideology that we are unworthy beings and provokes a subservience to those that seek to control and make up the rules.

Holding the correct focus whilst meditating creates positive progressive results due to the higher frequency that we are tapping into. The same applies to our bodies when we express through our body in this higher state of being, we will have marvellous bodily experiences. My body is also spiritual, everything we see, and touch is spiritual. I am a non-physical consciousness expressing through my magnificent avatar, my body. And this cannot be something terrible, on the contrary, it is the very core of what I have come forth to do.

'I am the creator of all my circumstances, the best and the worst'

To me this feels empowering and feels far more liberating than feeling doomed or condemned for life due to some past Karma from a previous life. Looking back, I could see this pattern very clearly. I had created all the good fortune but also all the mess in my life, I had of course not created any misfortune on purpose. I had responded to circumstances in a default mode instead of shaping them intentionally, because I did not know better.

Perfectly Imperfect

It is okay to let people know the things we do not like and point to things we love instead. While it may upset some, it also resolves uncomfortable situations. The saying goes,

'Those who mind don't really matter, and those who matter don't mind.'

I used to feel guilty about many things, I was expected to become that perfect person everyone desired me to be. That made me feel fearful of doing something wrong, I was replaying feelings of blame, criticism and guilt in my mind. Without knowing that every time I was thinking such thoughts, I would attach the emotion connected to those thoughts more firmly to my cells. I did not realise that replay was creating beliefs that were damaging to my emotions.

I had reached a point where I had some cleaning up to do. In the first instance, I believed I should resolve those uncomfortable memories by asking for forgiveness. After all, this was what I had been taught throughout my life from various quarters and heard it again in the course of my Brahma Kumaris studies. I made a list of what I believed I had done wrong, a bit like a confession. I felt guilty about various things, some less significant than others. I gathered up my courage and contacted people who I thought I needed to apologise to for things I believed I had done wrong in the past. However, what happened astounded me. Some did not remember or if they did, did not perceive any wrong had been done. I had considered myself in the wrong for no reason. I believed I was working on forgiveness to deactivate the hurt I was feeling but what I had done instead was to reactivate the memories of blame. This ideology of forgiveness did not serve me well at all. Asking people to forgive me was like asking to reverse something, it is impossible to modify what has happened, I could not change the past. What was done was done. I just had to let it go and forgive myself, a far more difficult task.

We all make mistakes, it is a part of living. Life throws lots of things at us, it is how we react that plays out to what could be a tragedy or a comedy. We are allowed to make mistakes, and we have the right to make the correction, sometimes an apology may be appropriate, yet we always have the right to a happy life, an error should not condemn us to a life of misery, there is always a solution to every flawed decision. When we feel hurt, we make judgments unaware that judging someone else is judging an aspect of oneself. However, when I find myself judging, it feels better to stop and let go without feeling any shame. When I let go, I am in a state of evolution, I am evolving my consciousness. There is no use feeling shameful over anything. Progress is achieved by learning to move away from judgement and shame. Maintaining self-respect and self-love is beautiful and the most important thing, when we love ourselves, we become powerful and beneficial to everyone around us, we are in tune and make the right choices intuitively and guilt is not part of this. God, does not need to forgive because there never was a reason to condemn to begin with. God will never determine anyone as undeserving nor do the universal laws. Infinity intelligence does not take deservingness into consideration, we are all governed by rules that are impartial, a non-judgmental mechanism that responds only to how one feels and vibrates. The more untroubled I became about self-condemnation, the more my frequency rose. The idea of forgiving someone always feels like it is about what somebody else did, but it is not, freeing myself from condemnation is about letting myself be who I am.

Aligning with my higher being will bring freedom and relief from blame and guilt. Forgiveness is never about the person I believed I had to forgive or be forgiven by. I am not anyone's judge, not even my own. Forgiveness was not essential, since my nature is to love and whenever I love, forgiveness is not needed. Clearly hating will never turn me toward love or happiness, appreciating myself will. Allowing myself to let go of blame and guilt is being kind to myself, loving myself is a form of self forgiveness.

It Is All for You

Access to infinite knowledge that creates our realities lies beyond religious boundaries, everyone has access to this endless creativity. Today the studies and disciplines of the Brahma Kumaris seem like a distant memory of the past. Having been a part of this spiritual organisation provided a space to practise and harness my intuition. My spiritual growth and experiences were not the result of being part of an organisation but were because of the practise, attention, and intensity I had given to my own development. Being in a spiritual environment allowed me to stay focused, it was an adventure where I made acquaintance with many mysterious people, I learned about customs I never knew existed. Those precious hours of meditation, conflicting encounters and experiences while exploring, equipped me with a higher level of focus and concentration, clarity and wisdom which have led me to new knowledge and understanding. Though it was my own extensive and continuous desire which drove me, a desire that lay outside of any religious body. The year 2008 was when I decided to leave the Brahma Kumaris, this was also the time I discovered the universal law of attraction, living a monastic life of a BK sister was extraordinary in many ways, yet it was also one of the most significant contrasts that I experienced. I found mind blowing knowledge but also contradictory doctrine. Questioning those contradictions led me to understand that I am perfectly capable of knowing how to figure out my own truth. Our core nature is happiness, this is something we already possess. All one needs to do to experience this joy is to unlearn all those restrictions and conditions we picked up along the way which do not allow our natural flow of joy, thoughts, and love.

Whilst taking assistance in conjunction with self-healing I experienced many shifts releasing one layer after another, as my anxiety drifted away, I felt what it meant to be free of fear, as my energy was transforming and stabilising, my life around me started to change. I had grown into a better version of myself, my thoughts felt different, I reacted and behaved differently, I started to like myself, I transformed into a new me. Had I come to this point, because of all that I have done, or would my path have led me to this point no matter what? I will never know. What matters is that I reached here and that there is more expanding to be done.

Empowering versus Controlling

My pursuit of happiness has taken me on so many detours, the goal to attain enlightenment seemed impossible, but I never gave up investigating. As a child, I imagined a man who I claimed to be my real father. I believed that my parents were not my real parents and were only temporary parents. My dream father was altruistic, extremely wise and masterful in living life, he knew how to make every moment more beautiful than it had been before. He was knowledgeable and possessed powers that were ruled by love. Being around him felt blissfully satisfying and fun, he would guide me skilfully through life, teaching me how to develop my own hidden powers. That was my idea of how I would experience enlightenment as a kid. Later I was taught that enlightenment is achieved through spiritual effort and discipline. Today I have formed my own conclusion of enlightenment. It is not some sort of mental state I had to achieve through discipline when I would be forever illuminated. Enlightenment comes from those moments of bliss when I have absolute clarity of what wellbeing is, a state of complete knowledge, where I can feel the power of divine source streaming through me and through everyone around me.

'Be careful not to become so heavenly that you are useless on Earth.'

Most of us believe enlightenment is unattainable. When anyone expresses a limited opinion of what is possible, it always comes from their own restricted viewpoint. Limited experiences of the past have nothing to do with what is possible in the future. We are wiser and more resilient than we give ourselves credit for. Our growth is an individual process based upon where we stand now. Only I know where I stand in comparison to where I want to be, only I can understand if I desire change, my change is bespoke to me. I am completely capable of writing my own book of what works for me or not.

Like every religion or spiritual organisation, the Brahma Kumaris believe that their teachings are the highest and most noble. The aim of a BK is to attain full soul consciousness. A state of being conscious of the self, as an eternal soul within a physical body while withdrawing from the influence of the bodily senses. This level of purity is required to enter the 'golden age' a heaven on Earth in the future reserved for followers of the Brahma Kumaris doctrine. I had allowed myself to be influenced depriving myself of my own intuition. Although, my meditative practice amplified a great urge to express myself creatively. I would stop myself from acting upon those impulses, even when an opportunity presented itself. Instead of following my higher consciousness that was pulsating through me, ready to express itself. I kept depriving myself of my own creative expressions, as I had allowed myself to be influenced by teachings that demanded withdrawal from all desires.

'By obeying the dictate of others, we turn into followers of someone else's dreams, instead of creating our own.'

Ruled by fear and convinced of one's imperfection the feeling of unworthiness is running rampant in our society. Instead of trusting our inner guide we learn to be led by others who decide what is right or wrong on our behalf. I observed how those who made up the rules were unhindered by them, disregarding the rules they made up to control others. The moment I start following somebody else's directions, I am no longer pursuing my truth. While practising the BK beliefs, I denied my natural senses to express myself through my body, I found myself wholly withdrawn from the physical world. I had taken my practice so severely that I was living in an altered state of mind. Although my meditation was an adventure and blissful, I found myself lost whilst in my body conscious state unable to function in the system that was dictated to me. Body contact had become alien to me, isolation had become the norm. I became somehow desensitised to people's emotions. The truth was that this part of the BK's teaching did not serve me well. It felt restrictive, I was forced to deny my creative expression, the core of who I was. This did not create the life I had hoped to achieve. A turning point had occurred when I realised that the BK teaching, I had faithfully followed would need to be dismissed entirely.

This physical world I was living in, was already filled with incredible beauty and abundance. I was born with an incredible functioning body, equipped with the most magical senses, and a mind that could create a 'golden age,' right here and now. So many try to generalise and come to solutions that are supposed to work for everyone, which is not possible. People can have their own views about all sorts of subjects, some are great, and many are controversial. Accepting diversity does not make anything wrong. Yet anyone who lives with anger and has the need to control beliefs or spiritual practices of others is not nourishing the soul. The right teachings are those that empower us, not control us. There will always be diversity in the world. We are made to be different, and there is no right or wrong way of living our life. I am the only one that can discover what is best for me. It is impossible to sculpt one philosophy to suit all, my life is my making, I can figure it out and live it my way, any mistakes I make are mine and will always bring forth new ideas which will help me clarify what I truly want. I can observe and choose, and believe in the things that will help me to align with my higher self. That is my natural state of wellbeing. Every thought has a value, regardless of what others perceive as right or wrong. The World simply cannot bend over backwards far enough to please everyone. We live in this World of such diversity where there will always be something that may offend someone.

Look at television news and documentary productions. They feed us with so much garbage. Video clips cut and edited to distort facts to misrepresent and promote violence under the guise of compassion, presented to make us feel pity and concern for the suffering and misfortune of others. What does this truly achieve? It makes us feel hopeless and worse it desensitises us. It creates a collective consciousness where we become accustomed to violence and deception. This is a fundamental misunderstanding of what compassion truly is. For some reason, many believe that compassion is observing an unsettling situation and becoming upset by it, if I allow myself to drown in the sorrow of others, or upset myself about a situation to please others, I become a victim of my own careless thinking this is disempowering oneself. For me compassion is an alignment with my own powers first and then I will project love, wisdom and knowledge, so that I can give the right attention needed to any issue, this is how to be the pillar for others to hold on to. Others around us will feel this to be uplifting, a sensation of real comfort that also carries understanding. This strength and wisdom is not bound by age or experience, it comes from the clarity that flows through us when we are in alignment with our higher self. This is the point when knowledge is easily accessible.

This can be achieved regardless of age. I have observed this in the old and young. Young people, also children can be extremely wise, they intuitively know how to love, when they anchor a pure alignment to their higher consciousness.

Worry the Downward Spiral

Worry is a downward spiral it creates a momentum of repetitive thoughts that play up the worst case scenario in the mind thus robbing us of creativity. It occurs when we are out of alignment with our higher self. Thinking about adverse outcomes repeatedly reinforces beliefs that change one's physiology. Fear based beliefs are emotionally draining. The human mind absorbs with the same ability as it does when events happen for real. The brain does not distinguish between what is imagined and what is real. Therefore, whatever we imagine good or bad affects our whole being, if we play out imagined events in our mind, it is like having that event actually happen. Imagination is so powerful that this same brain function that allows us to accomplish miracles can also potentially gradually destroy our lives. I would worry about so many things believing circumstances were out of my control, the stress would convince me that I am the only one trapped or rejected, though this is not the case, everyone experiences suffering at some point in their lives.

It is said that suffering has a purpose, this was the last thing I wanted to hear when I found myself in the midst of it. It took some convincing to view the challenge in my life as an opportunity to move into something new. Worry was a spontaneous reaction that made me feel anxious when fighting against an uncomfortable situation. But once I learned to release even a little of it, I definitely had an easier ride. I diligently worked myself out of fear and worry. I learned to listen to my inner whisper reaching out to me persistently telling me to align with my higher self.

'Do not invite anyone to join you in your pain, as it won't make it easier for you or them, no matter how deep your pain, there is always a stream of wellbeing flowing, that awaits to uplift you.'

Just because the solution is not visible yet, it does not mean that it does not exist. When one allows oneself to turn thoughts even a little towards something that feels better, a relief will be felt, a series of untainted thoughts will move us towards alignment and with it comes the solution. Being aligned makes one many times more powerful than someone who is not, as there is no self-doubt and no contradictory thoughts to disorientate us.

Fear the Paper Tiger

I was being pulled downwards, falling deeper and deeper. I was afraid, I was stumbling through a black hole. My body was plunging like a heavy rock with accelerating speed. I felt faint, and my thoughts were out of control. I could not hold one clear thought, and it seemed that the more fearful I became the faster I was tumbling. I was plunging into the unknown into a dark downward spiral. 'Change direction,' I heard a steady voice saying. 'I can't, I am falling too fast.' I shouted in panic. 'You are afraid, that's why you are falling.' The voice responded. The more I was trying not to be afraid, the more fearful I was becoming. I was falling at the speed of light into fear, and I felt the fear so powerful that I lost control of all my senses until I hit a climax of surrender. I did not have to fight anymore, as I let myself fall. The dark hole I was spiralling down started dissolving, a soothing blue sparkling light penetrated through its walls, and I found myself floating in a stream that felt gentle and safe. My thoughts had slowed down and became more explicit as though someone was doing the thinking for me.

'Do not be concerned with fear, your storm is only as real as the belief associated with it. Know your path is always lit. Your purpose in life is joy and expansion, your happiness doesn't need to be earned, it is your birth right, wellbeing is available for you, you are worthy of the very best, let go of fear, and your path will light up right in front of your eyes in the most perfect way, allow yourself to flow with the stream of wellbeing, we are your guides and will always have your back, you are loved so very much. Trust your own experiences, focus on the light and love within you everything else will take care of itself, know your greatness, and bring it to yourself. Keep moving forward no matter how small your steps seem as you keep moving towards love. Look into the eyes of those you meet, you will feel the connectedness of all that is.'

My eyes gently opened and I fully awakened, my heart was softly pounding from the excitement of this vivid dream, *'where had I been?'* I had landed safely back in my bed and the sun was shining brightly through my large bedroom window. I felt eager, relieved, and somehow changed like I had been equipped with a new tool.

I had become so used to walking through life with an unpleasant feeling in the pit of my stomach, that it felt normal. I had harboured a sense of fear and abandonment from my childhood and teenage years, being told off, yelled at and slapped, by strict teachers, parents, and sisters. Those events became triggers for fear for a sensitive child and were exaggerated by the traumatic losses I lived through, the emotional impact these events had left were never addressed at the time, and I had carried them into my adulthood without noticing it. By feeling fearful, I would naturally attract situations and circumstances which exacerbated this fear. The more afraid I felt, the more nervous I became. I was in a constant battle over my emotions, believing I had to be courageous to overcome my concerns, hence I was often viewed as the strong one. Though being brave would not make the fear go away, what was required was a subtle shift in energy.

'Those moments when I experienced loneliness were not because I felt alone. They were because I felt fearful of life.'

Fear is a state of mind that can shut down the immune system. Understanding fear helped me to neutralise this emotion, instinctively we know our own worthiness when we feel inadequate and doubt our worthiness, fear arises, then thoughts of happiness seem to be out of reach.

I managed to let go of many fearful beliefs by diffusing circumstances that I thought were frightening, by questioning them in an optimistic manner, our minds work like a search engine. I would ask myself a question, in an attempt to reach for a better feeling, an answer would always be delivered. I noticed when asking how to feel better I would create a small opening, a receptiveness allowing a better momentum of feeling to kick in. It acts like a tuning fork assisting with the tuning of a better feeling frequency.

Fear is the lowest vibration in the universe and fear is the worst enemy of our immune system, fear takes away our power, when we are in fear, we will become sick, we are always creating the reality we focus on. The devastation that has been and is occurring around the world may justify the uncertainty so many people feel. Though when we look at them as an opportunity to break through those fear based boundaries. We can shift to whatever brings comfort and create a steady frequency in our bodies, when we clean up the old, we create the space for the birth of something new, each one of us harbours an ability to shine through any upheaval.

Power of Sleeping

I woke up with excitement every morning, in anticipation of going through the day as quickly as possible so I could get back to bed and sleep to continue my dreams. I must have been about eight years old and voluntarily went to bed early every evening. I had figured out how to take charge of my dreams. I manipulated them to whatever I wanted them to be. I created the most adventurous vivid dreams, I was creating movies whilst sleeping, my emotions were the script. Whilst dreaming I was aware that I was dreaming. Whatever I was feeling manifested immediately and created all the characters and settings around me, I was the director of my dreams and also the actor in them. Whenever anything happened in my dream movie that I did not like, I would take control and change the script by adjusting to something that felt better. That little girl's nights had become more exciting than her days.

I always believed that I dreamed all night long, when really, dreaming happens very quickly, when one is in the process of waking up. The timespan of dreaming is usually only a few minutes long sometimes only seconds. One can get a lot of clarification from dreams, dreams are affected by the beliefs and emotions we feel. The experiences in my dreams were usually a pure reflection of what I was thinking and feeling while being awake.

After the death of my family, I used to have the same bad dreams on a regular basis. I would often wake up crying, feeling abandoned, rejected, and left behind by my family and friends, feeling angry at the unfairness of it all. I dreamed those dreams for years, waking up emotionally tormented, until I learned again how to guide myself to dream well. We tend to wake up to the vibration we had going before we fell asleep. The evening and morning can be powerful times to set a focus on how we want to feel when we wake up. I attended to programming my mind in advance every evening by writing many pages of words that would trigger uplifting feelings. My bad dreams became fewer and eventually I had dreams where I started waking up laughing.

I have always believed that when I sleep, I am resting my body, yet sleeping is much more than that. Every time I sleep, I align my vibration, my body recharges to its natural alignment, while my consciousness connects to my higher self. We can all do that. The sleep process is an automatic alignment with our higher consciousness. When we sleep, we withdraw from this third dimension. During our slumber many of us go travelling, into other dimensions, to realities that lie beyond Earth, yet when our consciousness returns into our Earthly body we mostly do not remember, as this 3D matrix is set up to make us forget.

Sleeping has a great advantage that goes beyond rest. Every time we wake up, a new day provides an opportunity for a fresh start, during sleep we stop any negative momentum we may have picked up during our day. Sleeping is a high vibration state, the short transition time from sleeping to waking up is the moment to focus on appreciation and to welcome oneself back into the body recharged, during this time the mind is most receptive and will set the mood for the day.

As a Brahma Kumari, I would feel guilty if I slept more than six hours, or had a nap in the afternoon. Conversely, as I learnt and understood how powerful and essential my sleep was, I let go of those rigid disciplines, they had served their time, and I allowed myself to sleep whenever I needed it. I found that naps would bring me back brighter, more alert, and I could achieve things in a much shorter period.

Dimensions

'Do you see how marvellous your Universe is?' I replied in surprise, 'Are you me in my higher form?' I could feel the voice smile, It continued explaining, 'Your Universe is a multidimensional reality vibrating in octaves. Your planet Earth is set in a cosmos that consists of twelve layered dimensions.' I asked, 'How do we get to those places?' The reply came, 'Those dimensions are not places but are states of being these Universal dimensions are eternal and form the basis of this Universe, they are realities that continuously resonate within the exact frequency. Each dimension differs, and are separate from one another. Earth is a third dimensional planet, within this reality. You the perceiver can experience the first to the third dimensional lower frequencies. Then there are the frequencies that exceed the third dimension these are the higher frequencies. Any being that is resonating in a lower frequency dimension cannot perceive existences in the higher dimensions, while higher beings can perceive all realities in every dimension below them. Five dimensional realities and above are benevolent realms. It is not to be viewed that those benevolent beings have any form of hierarchy over humans, it merely explains the frequency realms of celestial beings or Starseeds that originate and recite in the higher frequency dimensions. Those beings can see, know, and observe the lower dimensions as well as their own higher dimension and can function in multidimensions at the same time.

This Universe has various levels of vibration, the lower 3D dimension is dense, and the manifestation process is slower, the matter is more solid in its forms. The human race resides in the third dimensional reality and is controlled and governed by fourth dimensional beings that do not have the best interest for humanity. The intelligence of humans has been undermined, the human race is far smarter than their leader's hence they are being suppressed. Humans can ascend into dimensions beyond the 4D, your intellect is what their fear is. Humanity awakening is their end of the reign. Your enlightenment is the victory *over darkness, the shift of Earth is inevitable and imminent, yet the shift must start with yourself.*

The higher frequency dimensions are 5D and above, they vibrate at a higher rate and are lighter, the manifestation process is faster or instant. Most religions worship a God, which is, in fact, a galactic being from technologically advanced galactic civilisations. Each Galaxy is a directive to a spiritual council of wise and beautiful benevolent beings.'

'Wow, I need to get my head around that!' I expressed, 'Why is the council not intervening when bad things happen to the planet?'

'As you have chosen those experiences and you have free will. Yet still, the Earth's planetary council decided that humans on Earth are to be assisted. Because the destructive agenda that is occurring on Earth was pulsating through the Universe and affecting the neighbouring galaxies. The dark agenda needs to cease, assistance is now being given to help humanity come to unity. Humanity is being called to awaken and raise the collective vibration, to transform the grid systems of the Earth.

Work on your competence shall outsmart those who have taken control over you. Develop your human powers through meditation, breathing techniques, high vibrational nutrition, and exercise. These are your instruments to become powerful. It is easier than you think, you have been under mind control, that is how they outmanoeuvred you. Now is the time to turn the tables, humanity currently stands on a threshold, you all must raise your frequencies and unblock your energetic information centres and your Chakras. If they are blocked, the exchange of information is disrupted, your chakras direct and receive communication from your higher intelligence, unblocking them is your healing process.

You all have learned of the Schumann Resonance Frequencies. The different Universal dimensions can be measured in the same way by Hertz resonance that equal the state of consciousness. Your Earth's dimension is the 3D frequency that resonates with 7.810 Hertz, the 4D frequency resonates with 1230 Hertz and the 5D frequency resonates with 40100 Hertz.'

I enquired, 'But who determines who is to live in each realm?' The reply came, *'You do, each soul chooses according to the experience they wish to explore.'*

'If I understood correctly this would mean the Earth is a lower frequency planet with a harder living experience, is that right? But why would I or anyone choose to live in a low vibration dimension if it is so difficult when there are other choices?' *'To gain experience, so that your consciousness can expand into new experiences. Understand that you are an eternal being you have always existed, and you will always exist your expansion is endless.'*

'Why do we need to expand?' I queried, *'Expansion is a choice, if you choose not to expand, you will continue the same life where you left off. Your existence will continue to loop in the same or lower density planets. You pick the polarities to explore, to learn from those experiences and that in return leads you to a new level of dimensional growth. When you took birth and entered the third dimensional reality, you came forth knowing that you would dormant your memory of your multidimensionality to experience a single existence, not remembering that you are a part of a greater consciousness that is known as God amongst you, or also denoted as Source who is pure love.*

You knew that Earth is a place that was being claimed by beings that misuse their powers, you also knew that this was part of the three dimensional experience you chose. You knew there would be challenges that you would face, regardless you chose to enter Earth through the birth canal. You took that risk to be part of a greater plan. Your core beingness consists of 12 linear DNA strands. However, on Earth, you can only attune yourself to the frequency of two DNA strands. Simple creatures like bacteria have just one long, circular piece of DNA made up of two intertwined DNA strands. So, therefore, their experience remains one of the first dimensional frequencies. In humans, the two double helix strands that are intertwined like a spiral staircase are currently activated. While your other DNA strands are dormant. Each DNA strand reverberates at a different frequency synchronising dimension like a radio bandwidth would do. As your consciousness elevates, you will awaken your dormant strands that scientists call junk DNA. By raising your frequency, you will gain access to advanced talents such as telepathy, healing powers, and other phenomenal abilities, and you will start to remember who you truly are. 3D humans are not aware that they are third dimensional, they cannot yet perceive their divine abilities that lay dormant waiting to be awoken.'

'What greater plan?' I questioned, *'You soon will remember, know the work you do on yourself assists the whole. Keep steadfast in divine timing, you will activate the light within you. You are in the process of awakening and the plan is being revealed as you proceed.'*

The voice gently faded, I felt as if I was softly placed back into a denser reality, I found myself sitting in my armchair, where this journey had begun, in awe of what I had learnt. My body had gone nowhere, and yet I had travelled to places beyond my Earthly comprehension.

One Who Believes in Miracles Is a Realist

I was jumping into the azure sky one sunny morning in London's Hyde Park. I was learning how to fly, my body felt elastic and as light as a feather. I projected high into the heavens as if hurled by a slingshot. I felt happy and free enthusiastically waving at the miniature people below, some just strolling and others walking their dogs quietly enjoying the day. I hoped that they would look up and admire my high jumps. I glided smoothly back to the ground and prepared for my next spring. I adjusted my energy a jot then propelled myself even higher into the air. I gently dropped back down to the ground and immediately jumped again but with more precision, my spring each time stronger, taking me even higher.

Finally, I stayed up and I was flying. I had complete control, navigating my body through the blue skies, looking down at the people with their tiny dogs wagging their tails. Some people started to notice me and were looking up and waving. I could read their thoughts, *'I wish I could fly too.'* They were not deprived of the ability as I knew those people could fly too. If they would focus a little and adjust themselves they could also access the same energy that projected me skywards. I was gliding through the air, inhaling oxygen so pure, it felt delicious passing through my lungs. I was navigating myself with precision through the cooling breeze every move of my body was synchronised with the elements that carried me through the skies. Knowing that I could fly felt normal, it was like knowing I could drive a car. I did not need to talk about it, I had been happily flying every morning for three days.

Later as I was walking towards my home passing a beautiful sunny garden square, I suddenly felt the lightness of my body fade away and being pulled into a denser energy field. I felt confused and disoriented for a moment, my steps slowed down, my body felt more solid and heavy like I was walking through deep mud, then it normalised. I had adjusted, my surroundings had not changed. Had I jumped timelines to a different world or had I been sharing consciousness with an eagle? I caught my thoughts, wondering, had I truly been walking around for three days believing that I could fly?

Swapping Timelines

I heard a familiar voice behind me, *'Do you know who you are?'* I curiously turned my head and looked over my shoulder, yet no one was there. As I faced forwards, I found myself standing on the edge of a solid crystallised white stone surface, surprised I jumped back in fear, I gazed into an infinite drop that lay below me, the sight gave me vertigo, I took a deep breath to regain courage. I stepped further back to identify what I was standing on, I looked around and saw the surface projecting out from far away, I could not see the beginning or the end, it stretched into infinity. *'Where am I?'* I responded, dismissing the question and hoping that the voice would show itself to me. *'Do you like to live a life on the edge?'* The voice spoke again, this time it sounded closer. I felt a feeling of fear working itself up my throat. *'Do not be afraid,'* I heard the soothing voice say. *'Trust yourself, take a jump, let go of the edge.'* 'I am afraid,' I replied. *'There is nothing to be afraid of, let me show you.'* The voice explained. *'You are in between dimensions, here time is not linear as you know it to be on Earth. All your past lives, and future lives are concurrent in the present moment. The only reality is the space and moment you are perceiving in this now. This may not be easy to conceive from your three dimensional levels of consciousness, though as you are also operating at higher levels, this conception of no time should feel familiar to you once it is declared.'*

I felt a shift in energy and out of nowhere, I was surrounded by three different versions of myself, curiously walking around me and inspecting me, those versions of me were whispering to each other in an amused manner, *'She is almost me,'* I heard one say, *'well she is close to me too,'* responded another. The third one added, *'and not too far from me either.'* 'Who are you?' I asked, continuing, 'and why do you look like me?' They smiled and responded together *'We are you, we are the many versions of you. You have created us, we are the expanded form of yourself, we exist from your perception as a possibility, until you are ready to align and match your energy up with us. Then you become us, there are many versions of you, in variable dimensions existing in many different forms. We are the next closest match to your current frequency.'*

As I was listening, they were passing through me, placing themselves inside me, to show me how they felt. One after the other then all at the same time, those versions of me felt appealing like an advanced more perfected version of myself. Yet each version had different vibrational characteristics, of strength and personalities, but somehow, we were all the same, they were floating into and out of me and each other. As they were passing through me, I felt everything they were. I was able to see myriad layers of different versions of myself that represented possibilities based on the nearest available frequency that could match my current vibration, each version of me described a different timeline. None of those lives were past, present or future, time turned out to be this big illusion that we as a collective were holding in place.

I asked, 'How is this possible? I have been taught and accepted that time is linear.' The wise voice resumed, *'time as you know it on Earth has been invented.'* As the words concluded, my whole concept of time started to change like the press of a button. Time was not anymore what I thought it was. The counting of seconds, minutes, hours, days, months, years, dissolved into a flexible experience, time was not constant, it became the experience itself and I was the one to choose which experience to have. I was the one that got to jump into my next reality, to live out each experience.

I was witnessing my multidimensional beingness. My higher consciousness the grand conductor, was connected to a divine energy form which may be seen as God who is fully aware of all aspects of myself which had split into incarnate forms and then split itself again and again, multiple times, all were one, I was everything and everyone.

It felt like a dance, we were in a rhythm until they slowly faded away, *'Let go of the edge and allow the current to take you to who you really are,'* I heard them speak from a distance. I found myself standing firmly on the edge again, but this time it felt different, my fear had subsided, and I wondered why I was hesitating on the rim when I could fly. I did not belong there anymore, a feeling of relief came over me. Now that the fear was gone, I could freely jump and fly into my next timeline, away from the fearful edge, trusting in the current that was carrying me, skilfully manoeuvring me through multidimensional realities.

156

Capable of Great Things

"If you want to find the secrets of the universe, think in terms of energy, frequency, and vibration." Nikola Tesla

Activating our superhero capability. You and I live within a dimension that operates according to the natural law of magnetic vibrational attraction. I first discovered this law through a documentary and by reading numerous scientific and philosophical teachings. Understanding this law changed my conception of life, it was the answer to my constant questions, it resonated with me supporting my deepest beliefs. For the first time in my life, I had found a form of learning that symbolised freedom. It was not asking me to let go of my ambitions or dreams or to become something that someone else had dictated as the right thing for me. I discovered an immutable law, The Laws of Vibrations also known by many as The Law of Attraction.

The Law of Attraction is the base of everything in this world, it is a consistent factor in all things, both physical and non-physical, which respond to all that is vibrational. Everything on this planet has a vibrational frequency. We are vibrational beings, emanating energy through our bodies whilst we interact with the world around us.

Our emotions are the vibrational frequencies that determine how we experience life. So, what is my frequency and what is it made of? Understanding my emotional frequency and how it affects certain situations in my life was the most valuable teaching I learnt and was truly worthwhile acquiring. This perfect law that surrounds us responds to the continuum of our emotions like a magnetic pull, matching up circumstances that are a vibrational match to what we feel, emotions acting like tuning forks either positive or negative, are always emitting a wavelength. This means whatever it is, we feel, whether I am projecting intentionally or unintentionally, the universe's law of attraction will respond to it and deliver events and people that are a counterpart to my emotional vibrational projection.

Reflecting on my life I can clearly see those moments when I felt at my best, things seemed to be easily working out for me. I would find myself in the right place and one good event after the other would pop into my life like magic. We all have such moments in our life. This is the result of when a composed string of optimistic steady thoughts flows together producing a positive emotional momentum, that moves one into a high frequency zone, aligning us with more of the same. *'The better it gets, the better it gets.'* On the other hand, when I felt down, the lower frequency zone automatically matched me up with difficult situations one after another or even all at the same time, it felt like the whole world had ganged up against me. This is a negative momentum, *'When it rains it pours.'*

How quickly certain situations manifest in our life experiences depend on how stable the projected frequency is. The stronger the feeling, the faster the manifestation. One always attracts, either intentionally or by default. Since the law of attraction is an immutable law, I figured I might as well learn how to function within it. The idea that I could create my life by design rather than by default felt freeing. For the first time in my life, I started to take notice of how I felt and to my surprise, I was mostly feeling dissatisfied. I also notice the pessimistic mass media that was constantly bombarding us with bad news, dimming humanity's natural optimism. I would worry about many things in life though I rarely spoke about it as I felt unsupported and fearful and too embarrassed to admit it. Before I understood that the vibrational law existed, I was never able to figure out or explain why things were happening to me the way they did. After I learned how our own feelings shape our reality through the vibrational universal law, things suddenly started to make sense. I had discovered a tool that allowed me to take control of my life. I felt empowered, and life began to look different. I observed myself differently and felt immensely hopeful realising that I could do something about the events that I believed were out of my control.

Reaching for the Stars

Inspired, I decided to focus on starting my own business again. I was going to launch an environmentally friendly clothing range. I had my skills and my aspirations, but no budget and no clear idea yet as how to make it all happen, I was broke. I started to use my meditation time to visualise and feel the outcomes I desired. I experimented with some of the practices I had learnt in books I had studied. I wanted to find a way of earning an additional lump sum of £10,000.00. At the time, £10,000.00 was a figure I could easily relate to. I started visualising myself at my local banks' cash machine inserting my card and looking at a credit of £10,000.00. Simultaneously, I felt inspired to make a start on the designs, I was working on my drawings without really knowing how I would finance the development. I had almost completed my technical drawings, when I received an email out of the blue, from an unknown manufacturer informing me that he would be visiting London and would like to meet with me to introduce his family run clothing manufacturing services. We met, and we agreed to collaborate jointly. The manufacturer proposed to develop the samples with no advance payment until the collection was sold. I finalised my technical designs, created the patterns and sourced a selection of innovative environmentally friendly fabrics. And shipped everything to the manufacturer, back came a beautiful collection of about twenty pieces. The next step was to create the marketing material, I needed for the sales. The garments required to be photographed to be displayed in a catalogue for distribution. Whilst I now had a stunning collection of handcrafted garments, I was halfway there, but still did not have the finances to pay for the needed photoshoot production. Though I remained focused and continued to explore the options in my mind. I had a distinct idea of what I wanted, and I was not too concerned about my almost non-existent budget. I started my search and Googled for a photographer and connected with Paul Weaver, an ambitious website designer and photographer. At the time, Paul was in the process of establishing himself as a photographer, Paul had his own photographic studio.

I introduced myself and explained my project and asked about his fee, during our conversation, he explained that he had taken up photography recently and was just beginning to establish himself. As he was still building his portfolio and needed exciting images to add to it he agreed to shoot my collection. We decided to support each other and jointly planned a fashion shoot. We discussed ideas, Paul covered photography and postproduction, I provided the art directions plus my collection, we shared the cost of the makeup artist and model. Just like magic, we had brought together a creative team on a minimal budget. Our first fashion model was Karen Gillan, who later became a successful actress, in the Doctor Who TV Series. Our photoshoot resulted a series of astonishing photographs which I successfully used for the printed and digital marketing of my collection. A string of events materialised as a result. Our photographs were blown up and displayed at the Victoria and Albert Museum in London during a summit, celebrating the positive impact of fashion on biodiversity conservation. I was sponsored by the British Fashion Council, my collection was exhibited during London Fashion Week, and was picked up by fashion buyers and journalists. I was approached by a distributor who placed an order and paid a deposit of £10,000.00 into my bank account. A few days later, I found myself standing at a cash machine inserting my bank card and looking at a credit of £10,000.00, precisely as I had visualised it. All this had happened within a time frame of three months.

Well, that for certain was enough evidence for me, I kept visualising my next target. My exposure led to a connection with the United Nations Office in Switzerland. My label was exhibited during a world summit on innovative fashion in Geneva, put together by UNCTAD United Nations Conference on Trade and Development for redefining sustainability at an international seminar. It was attended by over 450 influential figures from World governments, private individuals and the luxury market sector. My collection started selling successfully in six countries. I had set myself a new financial goal of £150,000.00 that I maintained mentally focused on. Orders were flowing and a year had passed I had not kept track on the finances side of my business, until I received my year end company accounts showing a turnover figure of over £150,000.00, I had achieved my goal, and I did not even know it.

The business was thriving and tripling in sales, seasonally exceeding every financial goal I had set. It would have made a perfect fairy tale but suddenly, I found myself overwhelmed. My business was growing fast, I was unable to cope. My anxiety and stress spiked, and those feelings created obstacles, my success started to slowly vanish. I was on a downward spiral this time, and it all came to a standstill as quickly as it had begun. I couldn't stop feeling like a failure. Yet clearly, I had no doubt that I was living in a world of vibrational magnetic attraction. The evidence of my misalignment and alignment was mirroring itself to me. I was the one shaping my life. I had the choice to learn how to create my life deliberately, by filtering thoughts and sorting through emotions, or I could let everything happen to me by default and react to external circumstances.

Naturally I chose deliberate creation, this took training since the cells in my body were still geared up with stubborn negative beliefs from the influences I had acquired from this structural system we are locked into. It took some reprogramming, I experimented with various ideas to find out what would work. During my morning run I found that I was running faster and with less effort when I contemplated positive thoughts, by the time I had completed my run, I felt empowered. Sometimes old habits would take over, sneaking back into my mind. It took plenty of focus to maintain my positive emotions. When I had moments of anxiety, no matter where I was, I would retreat to a quiet place and calm myself until I had reached a point of relief. I paid attention to my thoughts and words and practised. I taught myself many things from reading books, watching, and listening to scientific documentaries that are never featured through any mainstream media channels. When my mind felt aligned to my higher consciousness, I could learn at an exceptional speed, I was experimenting with new ideas on my own, I was running a start-up business without enough budget to outsource things. Therefore, I had to do most things myself, even things I had never done before. Those were very creative moments. While making my first marketing video, I taught myself how to produce, edit, and apply special effects, using software I had never used before, to an advanced level within two weeks. Every new piece of knowledge I gained would expand my creativity and lead into entirely new territory.

Feelings

Bad feelings are a series of habitual negative thoughts that can be described as a false belief pattern, they act like indicators telling me my thoughts about myself are not true and that I am out of alignment with my higher self. Emotions serve us as our navigation system that let us know how we are doing.

Belief patterns are often established during our early childhood, they form our behaviour patterns unless we overwrite them with new belief patterns, they can remain with us throughout adolescence. These belief patterns can be positive or negative, depending on the influences and what we observed and claimed as the truth in our early life. I had somehow built a lot of negative false beliefs patterns about myself without realising it. One can imagine these beliefs as energy forms that operate in a default mode, wiring cells together like thick ropes. Shifting habitual negative beliefs to new positive belief patterns takes a little practice, it is like training emotional muscles. I practised often and used visualisation, and affirmation as tools to instil new ways of thinking. I had to unlearn virtually everything I had believed, commanding my mind and body to quantum leap into a new me was not something instant. In the same way, negative beliefs were not built overnight, shifting thought patterns happen by small increments. Maintaining a positive momentum over a long period was not the easiest thing to do.

I had built a moderately successful fashion business that had shot up in a short period of two years, only to witness a sudden hold. Of course, I felt I was thrown back to square one, and it seemed I had made no progress. Looking back, it is apparent that I had always made progress even when it looked like I had not, the business overall had yielded successfully, and I also had some fun while building it. Although it had come to a standstill some money was left in the bank.

I understood that the freedom and success I was seeking was an emotional journey, a major issue that required tackling was my anxiety. Whilst I appeared strong and determined I would worry about so many things, animals, children, people, the workers and their work conditions, our environment and so much more, I felt responsible for everyone. My anxiety was embedded within me. It kept bouncing up and down like a yoyo. Yet no matter how fearful I was about life I could not stop there. I had to make a comeback. I found myself stuck in a challenging situation. I felt a knot in my tummy tightening more and more, as my resources were running low, my anxiety rocketed to a level I had never reached before, my hair was falling out in bunches as result of my stress, luckily, I had a lot of it.

I had turned forty, and still felt that my life had not yet begun. I continued practising and explored further methods to allay my fears. I convinced myself that it takes practice to refine, sift and sort through emotions, affirmed to myself daily that this situation is temporary and there will never be an end of opportunities in life. I kept focusing, sticking to a high frequency diet, maintained my physical exercises plus spending time on daily visualisation.

So, I began again as before, I made a start working on my new design project without knowing how I would find finance. This time I created a vegan footwear collection, I got busy sourcing innovative cruelty free materials. Drew up a business plan and submitted it to various investors. After about six months, I received an unexpected call with an offer and a down payment of £50,000.00, a few days later I had the money in my bank account just as I had imagined. I developed the collection in Italy and received my first order from yoox.com.

Religion and Money
A Pass to Freedom?

'I did not like to be poor, yet I also knew it wasn't money that would make me rich.'

I had moments of success in my life, but I have also taken many dips. My ideas and thoughts were often viewed as too innovative and understood by only a few. I had many moments when I felt restrained and afraid, not knowing what my future may hold. Nevertheless, I was convinced my creativity, ideas and ethical values were needed and that I had to see them through.

The highest sense of satisfaction in life, which we do not always need money for, is to pursue our aspirations. Whilst I had focused on pursuing my financial goals, I noticed that in the process I was neglecting my pursuit of contentment, I was often faced with anxiety and stress. The experience made me realise many things. While financial freedom can be an important ingredient of happiness, it is not the only criteria for a satisfying life. Life becomes worth living when we have choices and the freedom to make life decisions, to be creative, and have access to a safe and beautiful environment. Abundance in a community is enriching, and our social connections are equally crucial. Therefore, our quality of life can only increase when we are all part of a supportive community of friends and family who are jointly contributing to a healthy environment, instead of allowing division, control and poverty of the people or destruction of this beautiful planet by corrupt global businesses, that are steered by a government with its own hidden agenda.

'The moment you feel that you do not need anything because you already have everything, all you desire will be at your fingertips.'

Bill posters and the tabloid press were directing me to worship those in power with big money, and it seemed like everyone around me had also been convinced, many adopt this ideal while justifying a distorted behaviour towards money and its real value. I witness people chase after money so intensively only to expose their greed, lies, and exploitative nature while jeopardising any valuable relationships in the process. I certainly did not feel it was much fun or satisfying to hang around such personalities for long.

Money is an essential factor in our daily lives. Most of us deal with money on a regular basis as our primary and vital tool of exchange in the game of life. Whilst money itself has little to do with happiness, the emotion we attach to it has. One should be skilful with money not to be ruled or deceived by it. When I had little money, life was full of disappointments. When I had a lot, it was my best friend and would buy me everything, even fake friendships. Indeed, it is a handy tool that can buy many comforts and many other beautiful things that enrich the enjoyment of life. It can seem like a brilliant exchange tool, certainly a lot easier than carrying bars of gold around or pigs and cows as a means of exchange.

There is a first time for everything in relation to new experiences, as young adults we select our studies mostly on the most common option available or based on the financial gain they may deliver, we start investing money and time. After spending years studying and accumulating a pile of debt, most people discover that being a banker, a doctor, a lawyer, or an architect turned out to be different from how imagined, or how it had been portrayed in the movies or on television. By the time we have grown into adults, we have been brainwashed to accept a life of financial mediocrity.

And how about this biblical mindset humanity is being fed? That money is the root of all evil and being poor is a virtue. Donating to the church, temple, gods, or spiritual organisations even if one cannot pay the rent, feed themselves or their families, it is seen as a benevolent act. These traditions are continuing in many modern religions and spiritual movements, selling liberation in the form of prayers, or holy water to the most vulnerable.

God does not need anyone's money, the source of nature is infinite, abundant, loving, and limitless. Therefore, any religion teaching that God needs your money is saying that they need your money to sustain their structure, so why not just say it like that? Such structures feed on dogmatic programming imposed by spiritual and religious organisations that deprive humans of self-empowerment.

The BKWSO being a very affluent religious organisation had a very similar tradition about money. Although their services and teachings are provided free of charge, the organisation was supported by their members that donate their time, lives, and money. Many of the BK seniors were frugal as this was part of their teaching. I felt uncomfortable about this part, I was strictly told to only give to *'Baba'* meaning to the BK Global House, the organisation. I did not mind giving to the BK Global house as my nature was one of generosity. I always had enjoyed gifting and sharing but restricting me to not share with others felt unnatural. Being a BK can make frugality a quality which was not my favoured one. Preaching that money was something negative, but donating all I had for Godly services was part of the BK teachings. we were told that this deed would create a favourable karmic account for our future lives. I virtually gave everything I had, most of all, myself the most valuable commodity.

Not many are able to think about money without clouding their thoughts with adverse emotions, most of us have been trained to believe in limitations. Some deprecate affluence priding themselves on being above materialism, whilst drowning in debt with little hope for the future, uncomprehending of what it truly means to be wealthy.

Money is not the gate to freedom it is a form of energy we use as a tool to trade in life. Like many, I was taught to count my success on a currency referred to as money, I used to measure my success based on how much money I had in my bank account. Since it never seemed enough no matter how much I had, I believed I had failed in every aspect of my life. Accumulating money seemed exhausting. I became convinced that I would never succeed in life as I simply could not accumulate enough money to make myself feel free.

By using this limited way of measuring my success I was depriving myself of my own freedom, I was so much more than a currency. Abundance and freedom are a form of energy, and therefore it operates under the same principle as attraction and resistance. Happiness is the means to riches, it does not work the other way around. Fortunes tend to magnify the individual's personality. Frankly speaking, if a person lacks values, riches will make them more of a detestable individual. If one lives by their values, fortunes are going to make that person even more virtuous.

Money is such a significant factor in our lives. We can get easily caught up in a worrisome feeling when there is not enough of it. Sometimes feeling resentful towards the success of others or playing down one's own worthiness of it will also hold abundance away. One must understand that those vibrations are contradictory to the necessary feelings of wellbeing and freedom. Wealth will not come through denying one's own right to abundance. A mindset that reflects the feeling of stability, security, and freedom will attract abundance. Worrying is one of the most unproductive thought processes that one can get trapped in.

Dare to Be Free

No one should be ashamed of having big aspirations or desiring freedom. Never allow the mass media to convince you that freedom is selfish, or that you owe an explanation for making your own choices, we are independent sovereign beings. There is no virtue in depriving oneself of all that is good. Our true nature is to be unlimited and free we are evolved to have an ability to tap into our own creativity.

Like most people, I was raised with the limited belief that I had to work hard to succeed in life. And most of the time I ended up doing just that, but it kept me struggling in a world of abundance, working myself to exhaustion in order to attain wealth, which did not quite work out. If hard work or education were the secrets to financial success every graduate or construction worker would be abundantly wealthy. It is not that wealthy people are more intelligent, better educated, or luckier. Many that accumulate wealth have little formal education. Having or not having a higher education or working hard are not the secret to success. The adoption of a specific set of beliefs and philosophies is. There are those that have been raised in an environment where abundance is natural and they develop the belief to expect abundance from an early stage. And others train themselves more deliberately aware of their focus and goals, in both cases, their way of thinking is geared up to attract success into their lives. The economy too is truly an individual experience, there are people that thrive in the worst circumstances, I too have succeeded in poor economic times and spiralled downwards in high economic times. When many around me were thriving, I found myself earning so little that I had to spend it all to sustain a decent existence.

We are all equipped to develop an optimum mind, self-education is key to acquiring new skills. Knowledge about the philosophy of frequency will equip one with the tools to become as free, happy or prosperous as one desires. One must stop listening to society and the bogus mass media to distinguish which source is the true authority, let your intuitive self-become your authority. To some this can be the hardest task. Allow your intuitive self to be the bearer of your experience, and confirmation of your own inner knowing. There are no leaders or followers within a highly intuitive union, only beings who are equal, sovereign, and free. This is how to become immune to brainwashing. It is not possible to brainwash an aware individual, attempts to do so will never work.

We are made to have never ending aspirations, there is just no end to what we can achieve. I choose to ignore everyone who attempts to undermine my or anyone's right to freedom, authenticity and creativity. No matter how much those naysayers attempt to convince me that I must follow the crowd or that I am being unrealistic. What they are doing is projecting their own limited vision of their fears onto those that aspire for greater things and freedom.

Today I am capable of perceiving success not merely on material belongings but more so on the development of my human spirit. The mastery of my emotional frequency is the golden key that grants me access to the vigorous, marvellous life I am able to achieve.

There should be schooling dedicated solely to the management of vibrations in every child's education. Vibration is everything, it matters more than anything else. Including what people may think about us.

Courage Is Contagious

United, we could have abundance and be free of money and rise above our financial system. Poverty should not exist in any society, everyone can be free. One may argue, it is a poor man's mentality that keeps him poor. While this is true, it is with certainty that even one that has known nothing but poverty from the day of birth can be deprogrammed and will shift with the right support of care, love, and trust, which every human being has a right to.

When we as individuals focus on freedom, abundance, and love, we expand, and this evolution creates a shift in the consciousness of the collective. The more we do things that cannot be purchased with money the more this economic enslavement system we are bound to will lose its power. There is so much to be discovered, explored, and experienced by widening our consciousness. The more of us who focus on honour, freedom and creativity, the more we will align to that virtue, and this will make our current financial system crumble so that It can be replaced with a structure that will keep us all free.

Abundance is natural and normal to the human state of being. The entire universe is enriched with limitless fields of possibilities. Nature is abundant, with ample infinite resources, nature does not hold back in fear of exhausting its resources, it provides generously and plentifully.

'The liberation we all desire is not the money, it lies in expanding our abilities'

Abundance is an emotional and vibrational adjustment that is a part of our wellbeing. Creating the life, we desire involves genuinely understanding and believing wealth is our natural state. Thoughts of scarcity and believing there is not enough money, jobs, love, energy, health, available partners etc, limits one's ability to access abundance or freedom. When we replace these thoughts of scarcity with believing in prosperity, liberty, and wealth, we come into alignment with our true nature, which provides us with an unlimited ability to create the wellbeing we all desire.

When we feel abundance there is no fear to give or share, any feelings of scarcity will vanish and we will know there is plenty to go around. When one gives freely, we will find joy in giving, if one is afraid believing that there is not enough of something or concluding that someone does not deserve it, one activates a vibration of shortage within oneself. Generosity is an emotion of abundance and love. When I truly love I become a natural free giver intuitively knowing where, when and what to give.

A psychologist who researched generosity discovered that it strengthens relationships and social ties. A vital ingredient in the creation of happy and lasting relationships is a genuine exchange of bountifulness, a form of kindness that can be expressed in many ways. Giving and receiving opens the gate to an enjoyable partnership, generosity is an extension of love. Understanding the needs of others and assisting in meeting those needs, opens doors to harmonious relationships. We all love people who have a generous nature and equally it is fun and satisfying to be one of them, generosity generates happiness. The more generosity in a relationship the more exciting it becomes, acts of kindness for no reason but just for the pleasure of it are beautiful forms of exchange, it will deepen affection for one another and provide a sense of stability and trust. Giving is only one part of the fun. Accepting and appreciating is just as valuable, I hear people downplaying compliments or praise when receiving a gift saying, 'You shouldn't have' or 'there was no need.' This is like telling the giver, 'I am not worthy of the love or generosity you have to offer.' By heartily accepting and appreciating kind words or gifts that come our way we allow abundance to flow.

Elevator to Happiness

Time does not heal all wounds, what heals is loving yourself, accepting yourself, addressing your emotional wounds and learning how to become free. There was always more growing up to do, no matter where I stood in life. As a teenager, I was guided towards a life of mediocrity by my parents and peers. This I was ardently opposed to, and I rebelled against it. I took many detours in life until I realised that cultivating wellbeing was the solution to everything. Wellbeing will manifest itself in many ways, but it is always governed by distinctive emotions that we can all feel and see, Joy makes us beautiful, our eyes shine, our skin glows and our bodies feel healthy, our minds seem clear and alive. When we are happy, endorphins produced by our body trigger positive feelings. Endorphins are distributed throughout our nervous system. I often felt anxious and sincerely desired to be free from it, so I would do all I could to learn how.

No matter how many philosophies of the greatest thinkers I read, unless I explored them myself, nothing would truly change or turn into something new. The only way of really knowing was through my own experience. My body learned to love exercising, swimming, running, stretching, dancing, singing and being close to nature along with a healthy nutritious vegan diet plus drinking lots of water. All these activities and disciplines surely triggered some pretty good feeling. Yet they would fade. Why would those moments when everyone feels so perfect not last longer? I loved my daily exercise, but even as a sport enthusiast, I could not run around the park all day long just to get my endorphins going, it would become boring at some point. So why did it fade? Joy fades because the focus shifts, and the focus shifts because it has not been practised to a level where it remains unshakable, because external matrix fear based influence is forcing it out of us. I was not prepared to be defeated by this programming.

My television was dumped a long time ago and newspapers were banned from my home. I was fully prepared to go the extra mile, to purge out all the subliminal influences that constantly surrounded me. I developed routines and rehearsed mental exercises to strengthen my wellbeing. I dedicated hours, days, and months of writing page after page of positive affirmations, applied self-hypnosis and created an entirely new reality of how I wanted to feel and be. I created recordings with empowering words, using binaural beats and isochronic tones that I would play back to myself daily and during sleep time. I also taught myself EFT tapping by reading numerous books about the subject, EFT stands for Emotional Freedom Techniques, it works a little bit like acupuncture but without the needles. Using my own finger, I tapped on specific points on my body whilst affirming specific words. I found it to be an effective anxiety relief technique. I explored further and researched NLP Neuro Linguistic Programming and booked myself a series of sessions with an NLP coach. It did not end there I also dived into exploring sound healing, a healing practice that uses specific sound vibrations such as Tibetan singing bowls, gongs, and tuning forks to sooth and help me shift. I continuously explored the alternative healing path and met with Reiki masters for energy healing and engaged in past life regression sessions. I read one book after another and like a sponge I absorbed knowledge to explore test and try. I stretched my imagination, to think out new ideas as how to generate more desirable neuropaths in my brain. I dedicated myself to self-educate about all the subjects I knew so little about. As I explored, tested, and discovered alternative approaches of how to heal my fears and improve my life.

Too much? obsessive even well maybe, but then again, I had signed up to live an extraordinary life and what I was doing was bringing me closer to this ideal. Being obsessive or extreme about wanting to learn something was right up my street. What some view as obsession, I see as dedication. Would I make mistakes in my explorations? of course and part of this education includes to learn how to be kind to myself, and dim self-criticism whenever I was not at my best, whilst figuring out how to shape myself and improve my life.

Friendships and Angels

'Sometimes it takes an overwhelming breakdown to have an undeniable breakthrough.' quote unknown

We all have an engine that breaks down from time to time, sometimes it even gets smashed and needs complete rebuilding. I had moved away from home and created new relationships in London. And when my 'engine' got crushed, I sensed that the support I was hoping for, from people I believed to be close friends, was not forthcoming. I felt embarrassed and uncomfortable realising that I had made the wrong kind of relationships and invested in false friendships. When we face challenges, we often feel vulnerable, and without the right support, we can feel lonely. My feelings of loneliness and inadequacy occur when I feel unsupported, it was my lack of self-love causing a feeling of not deserving support. Thoughts of not feeling good enough can be deeply ingrained. I could list thousands of reasons how such beliefs develop. From the many rejections one receives throughout life to how one is valued in society.

A classic misconception most of us have been brainwashed to believe is that worthiness is something someone else decides on our behalf, therefore I had to be confined to specific behaviour in order to be worthy, yet nothing is further from the truth. No one holds the power to determine anyone's worthiness. Self-worth is a feeling that is created from within. Babies and small kids have a natural sense of feeling worthy, that is why as kids we are so excited about life. We are all born with a healthy sense of self-worth. As we grow up, we start to lose that sense due to negative outside influences. We begin doubting ourselves when we are compared to others, measured, and judged by teachers, parents, or other influences that surround us. They pointed out our weaknesses, instead of encouraging us to build on our strengths. Those patterns form within us at a young age and if left unchecked deepen and continue into adulthood often unrealised.

The feeling of abandonment that I was experiencing made me revaluate my relationships and my connection to my higher self. And it steered me into reaching out to a higher divine source for support. The sustenance I received which came to me through this channel was invaluable. There is always somebody there to show us the way out. Even when we have created an environment where we feel we are not good enough to be loved or worthy of support, like I had done. We all need help at some stage in our life, and we should not be ashamed to ask. In my case, it was not the people I had invested most of my time with that genuinely cared or offered me their love and support. It doesn't necessarily have to be the people we thought were our closest friends or family that will be ready and available to love or support us when we feel at our lowest. When our asking is directed at God, our Angels, or the Universe many beautiful people will cross our path to be available for us, exactly when we need them, and provide the right help in precisely the way we need it. Sometimes those can be strangers, new relationships, or friendships that we formed in our past that pop back into our lives. To me, those people are angels even if they do not know it. Helpers will appear in magical ways, depending on our situation, often it will be more than one person to provide the support we need. Whenever I would look up into the skies reaching out to God, he always sent his angels in very unexpected ways. My job was to create the space and allow the helpers in. One person cannot always fulfil all areas of support we need. At challenging times, I accepted help from various people, in the subjects they offered and were able to make themselves available. Each one of them contributed in different ways. The support, love, and kindness I have received from those unique people who popped in and out of my life were the greatest gifts. They knew intuitively when support was needed, their generosity felt safe and provided the space where I could accept without feeling inadequate. When we succeed and get through our darkest moments in life, it is because there is somebody there to support us. I am convinced that the reason those people appeared or stayed in my life was that I trusted in God and his universal helpers.

Healing

'Look into the mirror and you will see the miracle you have been waiting for.'

It is not expected of anyone to be happy when one is in pain, when the burden feels too much, but one can move into hope and ask for assistance, comfort, and love. Our higher guides, our Angels are always by our side, when frequency dips too low, we no longer resonate with the higher frequency, our guides cannot reach us, they must wait for our permission to share energy to assist us, that is where healers come in between. You are never abandoned, while our guides cannot walk the path for us, they are always by our side, guiding us, loving us, supporting us. But one must invite them.

'You have to keep breaking your heart before it opens. The wound is where light enters.' Rumi

Unhealed wounds are energy pockets that are passed on from one generation to the next, locking us into the third Matrix, which is the lower frequency field, until someone of our lineage faces and disentangles them, it takes courage, focus and determination. This healing process breaks the cycle, stopping those energy festering vessels being passed onto future generations. When we heal and are releasing emotions, we are also releasing the thoughts and beliefs connected to them, we cannot heal by ignoring those feelings or pretending they do not exist. Therefore, feeling negative emotion does not make anyone less spiritual. Having a fit of rage does not mean that you will not be invited to your self-mastery party. As you work through each stage, you will reach a point where you do not look for the nearest escape to hide from the feelings and memories that are so hard to accept. You will want to heal them, face them, and become free. As we soothe our wounds, we practise self-love that moves us past our imperfections, this strengthens us to face the dark versions of ourselves, that is self-mastery.

I have witnessed the biggest hearts that gave unconditional love in the most unexpected situations, a stepmother that loved so consistently that I sometimes wondered where her unlimited love came from, a stepbrother capable of caring in the most challenging moments. And then those that disappoint and betray, my outside was, of course, a complete reflection of my own attraction point. I had created everything that was staring me in the face, the good, the bad, the beautiful and the ugly. My feeling of vulnerability and anxiety had attracted people who exploited me. My desire for justice had drawn people who assisted me in sorting it all out. As I stood in the midst of my troubles, I could not clearly see how and why I would recreate the same events over again, different places, different people, same circumstances. I started to recognise my pattern, I understood that I did not want to be the victim, nor did I want to be someone that needed rescuing. Living through all those experiences launched my biggest desire, to be free.

Healers are people who allow the energy of higher consciousness to flow through them in a way that guides, revives, and empowers. A healer's power stems from their ability to facilitate self-healing, to allow the universal healing power that every human being naturally possessed.

As I explored in this area, I met many people disguised as healers. A psychotherapist who believed her knowledge could heal away my deepest fear in one session, only to find myself listening to her sales pitch at the end of the first session. I also came across an EFT practitioner who had an emotional breakdown during my healing session, and the role somehow reversed with me helping her and paying a high fee on my low resources.

The fact that those 'healers' were still addicted to smoking and drinking alcohol reflected that they had not done the most basic work on themselves. A healer should be free from addictive substances before they can give others meaningful support. While such healers may have specific talents there is often a lack of stability, this is very likely to backfire negatively during treatments of those in need.

When we seek help and invest our trust, money, and time during our most vulnerable moments to come across professionals that are unstable, it does more harm than good. The rule of thumb is when it feels wrong, it is wrong.

I also crossed paths with exceptional master healers, who were not only gifted but also had a lifetime of self practice. They had eyes that sparkled bright, and projected an energy that felt stable and pure. Free from any addiction and with an unwavering connection to their higher self. They heal by releasing or transforming energy, knowing that they act as a conduit and vessel. Master healers are never concerned whether one is able to pay a fee in exchange for healing, their focus is solely on transforming the unwell to well while using all their resources appropriately and provide the full safety net to give a secure and dependable environment. They understand that abundance will flow according to their own vibration.

The Spirit Plants

There are so many components to living, and my discoveries never seemed to end, as I was learning about emotions I was healing and raising my vibration. I was restoring lost links to my higher self, a wiser version of myself, curing my past and future, my process continued, the braver and more stable I became the deeper it took me to face and clear all my hurts, I had my ups and downs in the process and life turned into a roller coaster at times, but the downs became fewer than the ups. One moment everything seemed to be going along smoothly, then the next, an emotional layer emerged that was lingering to be faced for release. Financial stress sneaked back into my life, and my anxiety spiked. I had jumped many hurdles, though this aspect was yet one more to be nailed. Freedom was clearly what I was looking for, and it required a solid foundation. I had to resolve my underlying emotional ordeals that were rooted in my lineage. Emotional energy patterns that were deeply ingrained needed to go, and I felt that I could do it with some help.

It was 2018, plant medicine was popping up all over, being promoted as a healing alternative for emotional stress. I was not a fan of any forms of outside stimuli, in fact I was opposed to taking any form of drugs or alcohol, or being a part of a culture where people gather together to indulge in psychedelic experiences and walk around with spaced out faces. A peculiar activity I preferred to keep at a distance. Nevertheless, medicinal plants were an exciting subject, and I was curious to understand their origins, so I dug a little deeper and investigated. A whole new perception emerged as I learned more about how psychedelic plants had been used for centuries as medicines, by indigenous cultures for healing.

Many indigenous cultures harness a connection with benevolent extra-terrestrial beings, believing medicinal plants such as psychedelic mushrooms and Ayahuasca are planted by those benevolent beings to assist humans to connect with the cosmic consciousness bypassing the amnesia that occurs when souls enter a human body.

The extent of the power those medicinal plants hold is sacred and still not fully known. Traditionally, only the most skilful Shamans and Healers who had been trained and were able to connect with the medicine core spirit would be qualified to administer the sacred plant as part of a healing ceremony. The dosage would be measured with utmost care, and it would only be provided when healing was required. Plant medicine was highly honoured and respected and only used for healing ceremonies. The Shaman would hold a safe vibrational space for the person and assist the clearing of dense energies that were in the way of the soul's healing process. The experience could often be traumatic or uplifting the spirit plant would determine the healing procedure. Shamans valued the spirit plants highly.

Psychedelics were not applied in the same way as in the modern Western world where they are commonly used illegally for recreational purposes to get quick highs in order to escape reality.

Psychedelics Plants have been researched by Western scientists who established that psychedelics used in a controlled application can improve moods plus giving a feeling of unity. Which would continue even after the plant's effects wear off. The analysis also concluded that psychedelics increase the connections between the brain's neurons and could repair and rewire circuits, with transformative experiences relieving anxiety as one example.

The use of most plant medicine is illegal in the UK. Nevertheless, I was intrigued, willing to travel, and experiment. Whilst researching I came across organisers that promoted plant medicine trips like a package holiday in rather large groups and uncomfortable surroundings. This did not seem appealing to me as a setting for healing. The last thing I wanted to do was witness people around me puking into buckets, clearing out some trauma whilst feeling vulnerable myself, so I dropped this idea.

Instead, I asked the universe to deliver me the ideal setting, I visualised a modern comfortable setting with the perfect spiritual assistance to provide the healing experience I was seeking, naturally the universe delivered. Several months passed and I met an energy healer, Liam who had travelled to Peru and had acquired experiences with medicinal plants. As I learned more about his history, I gained trust and felt that Liam was gifted and qualified to provide the secure setting I desired. The sessions were on a one to one basis. Liam was highly intuitive and aligned to receive communication with his and my spiritual guides, which he would consult about the healing process, my sessions were uniquely prepared under their guidance.

Spread across a period of 14 months, I attended six psychedelic mushroom sessions and one Ayahuasca brew, each healing session was six to eight weeks apart and was conducted in a supervised spiritual setting. I was instructed on how to prepare for each session that lasted about four to five hours. In my first session, I was offered a small dose of organically grown psychedelic mushrooms. To perform at its most potent level the mushroom must be harvested in a spiritual environment. The mushrooms were usually prepared as a tea or blended in a juice.

During trips, I wore an eye mask and would lie on a comfortable chaise longue with layers of blankets and cushions, my body temperature would always drop drastically during sessions. After each session, there were seven to ten days of integration time, plus aftercare. In between sessions I Intuitively felt a great urge to juice fast to assist with the energy clearing. I fasted in between every session. The plant medicine made me feel nauseous, I felt like puking most of the time, though every time I felt I was vomiting I was letting go of air instead, freeing myself from restrained energy. I received visions and learned how every emotion is connected to belief patterns from former life cycles. At one point, I felt famished, and an intense feeling of starvation overcame me as I had never experienced before. I was then shown how craving for nutrients was a result of deprived emotions.

My trips on the medicinal plants were no ordinary experiences and anything but a joyride. Out of all the trips my second one was the only one that did not torment me. In fact, this one experience was mesmeric and astounding transforming me entirely. It was the only session when I was supervised from a distance, Liam was unavailable, and I instinctively felt I would go ahead on my own. I was provided with two small doses to be taken two hours apart. I lay snuggled up under my soft blanket. I turned on an album of soothing meditative piano music that played continually in the background. My eyes were closed and covered by an eye mask that served to keep my focus internal. As the medicine worked its way through me, I lost all notion of time, the light layered mask that was resting over my eyes started to hurt, I adjusted it, yet it kept hurting my eye lids. *'How odd,'* I thought, I moved the eye mask to my forehead my eyes opened automatically, then my eyelids would not close. 'Well ok*,'* I thought, I'll keep them open, so I sat with my eyes fixed wide open staring at the altered space around me. My surroundings had crystallised, I saw codes forming in the room, beautiful crystal clear codes were hanging unified in the air. I found myself in the most magnificent space, the energy around me had transformed into something incredibly divine, the furnishings of the room which had been there at the start of my session were still in the same place but appeared more beautiful and crystallised, the colours had turned more vivid, everything around me had upgraded and had turned into a new magnificent sparkling clear world. As I sat in awe marvelling at what I was seeing, I received downloads, fascinating learning about the structural universe, the knowledge that was streaming into me was a marvellous vivid display of our supernatural abilities everything had transformed, to an ideal environment and culture. I was in a state of ecstasy as I was shown how our Earth had gone through a transformation, the ascension process. The old structure of the world as I knew had crumpled, the third dimensional matrix, that had been based on a web of lies and disinformation, had dissolved. The old Earth had been blasted with high frequency light photon gamma beams that carried divine frequency and had awoken humanity. These codes had triggered the blueprints of human consciousness, to transition from a lower frequency consciousness to a higher divine consciousness. The world had moved out of its corrupt dense dimension and shifted into a higher benevolent fifth dimensional frequency, a collective transformation had taken place. I had arrived in utopia, I was shown a divine royal court that was being assembled by highly evolved benevolent beings. As I sat in amazement and disbelief, out of my mini speakers, I heard the sounds of an angelic choir singing explicitly to me, music unlike anything I had heard before. I felt the vibrational waves of the tones welcoming me to celebrate my awakening. The sounds carried the imprint of an assembly of a divine order, performing a celestial symphony of tones that were alive directed at me, filling my space with captivating melodies. I felt adored, mesmeric humming reverberated through every cell of my body. I questioned, 'how was such splendour even possible?' I lay mesmerised in disbelief into the night listening

182

and learning until the high frequencies exhausted me, then I fell into a deep slumber. I awoke in the morning back into the old world as I knew it.

At that time, I could not fully grasp the significance of what I had experienced, it had occurred four hours into the session when the peak effect of the psychedelics was supposed to have subsided.

On the following morning, still mesmerised by the beautiful sounds listened to the evening before that where still imbedded in my mind. Intrigued, I searched my phone's music history to find the divine melodies that had echoed through my mini speaker the evening before. I did not own such an album nor could I find a trace of the choir on my playlist history, I was left in awe and somehow confused. This vivid experience had changed me entirely. 'Was it true? Was our Earth going through a collective transformation? Could this be real, was I the only one to know about this?'

Plunging into the Dark

Liam facilitated each of the following trips with the spirit plant, which were nothing like the magical trip I had experienced previously when I had sat on my own. The trips that followed were no joy rides. The intensity increased each time, waves of trauma purging through me, in between releases I had dialogue with altruistic and benevolent beings, who assisted in soothing the emotional trauma that purged out of me. The bond I shared with them felt profound and loving as though they were part of me, guiding me through my liberation and healing process.

Looking back at the session, I had conducted on my own, it seemed as though the medicine had given me a preview at of what I was heading towards. Yet it appeared there was still a chunk of energy clearing to be completed before I could reach the world I had glimpsed at.

As each of my psychedelic trips intensified nothing could have prepared me for what I was about to experience. The trips that followed were torturous, the word does not do justice to describe the trauma that was unleashed through me. The identity that represented Ivana the fashion designer was wholly broken down. My old programming was dismantled, and it was not pretty. My ego was fighting for survival, I was tormented it felt like I was dying a painful death many times over again.

Assistance was needed, I felt the energy work that Liam was undertaking, the guides spoke to me in pictures and telepathically showed me how they used Liam's skills as an energy healer to identify what needed to be released within my emotional field. I felt the relief and shift of the work Liam was undertaking as he stood close by me and manipulated the energies that surrounded me. At one point I was asked to be used as a portal. I gave permission, 'are you ready?' I heard a telepathic voice speak, 'of course', I replied confidently.

I had no idea what I had let myself into, the ordeal turned into my darkest of the dark, it felt as though I was being used as some sort of purge portal for all the suffering that had ever existed on Earth passing through me to be disposed of, fear, shame, guilt, hopelessness, any hurtful emotion human can experience at its worst, It was hell that words cannot describe, the telepathic guides had taken over the process and Liam was put on hold, I was calling out in distress. Whilst Liam was comforting me through the process, the densest and darkest forms of energy kept purging through me. I was on the edge of insanity, there was no escape, and it lasted for hours, it felt unbearable. I was under severe strain. One energy layer after the other made its way out, a thorough deep clean up through history and many lifetimes was being performed. I felt the roots connecting me to every human on this planet, going back generations an emotional web was filtering through me, I felt anxious, nauseous and sick.

Finally, it came to a halt, I felt exhausted to the point I could not even speak, then I was being soothed by the angelic beings who were my guides, a gentle healing took place, I received telepathic learnings, and I was shown the divine royal court again, a hierarchy of wisdom, love and kindness that would be ruling our new Earth.

After each tormented trip, I was convinced that I would never touch plant medicine again. I called out to Liam, *'please remind me to never do this shit again.'*

Yet my wiser self must have thought otherwise, as days proceeded, I noticed a change within myself, an improvement in my feelings and way of being, the horrific memories of the psychedelic trips subsided in the weeks following each session. I was only able to recollect a little of the distress but predominantly remembered the short final soothing moments of the telepathic communication with my spiritual guides, I felt new each time and the healing process seemed effective. I cannot explain, it seems insane, but after the memories of the horrendous darkness I experienced had faded, I was intuitively led to do it again.

As I was preparing to digest the medicine again on each trip moments before I felt horrified, the odour of the medicine caused memory flash backs, the smell and taste of the psychedelics made me want to puke. I burst into a cold sweat out of fear, yet I continued, why did I resume? In the midst of every session, I had regretted taking the plant medicine, believing the plant spirit had killed me regretting it deeply that I had swallowed it. I found myself jolted out of my body beyond reality where nothing existed but loops of trauma that seemed endless, with no escape, as I felt I was already dead, there was nowhere to go. I felt the most extreme forms of fear, the plant spirit took me into dense realms where I had no wish to be, I felt lost for eternity without any memory of existence or time, grasping for some though that could create some shape and bring me into light.

When eventually I found my way back into my body, Liam stood by to help, as the furniture in the room slowly reappeared, I felt the utmost relief and most grateful that something existed, I felt gratified to see the furniture again and that I had returned to existence back in my body feeling intensely grateful to be alive.

After this I was adoringly assuaged by divine beings. '*Why do I have to have such an experience?*' I asked exhausted. I was reminded that I had agreed to this work, I had come to assist with the energetic clean-up of the collective. In disbelief and shattered, I informed them that I wanted no part of this anymore. I expressed clearly that they should pick someone else for this foul work, or they should do it themselves. They disregarded my complaints and encouragingly whispered.

'*We cannot walk the path for you, yet be assured your will for freedom is greater than your fear.*'

As the terror of the last trip faded from my memory, weeks later, I confidently was again drawn to take the Ayahuasca brew. We had anticipated that this trip would be the final one and were hoping for an easier ride and yet it was the cruellest of all. It felt as if my mind was being taken apart and reconstructed, a confusion and disorientation that I can only describe to insanity took place it seemed to go on forever, I deeper regret for having drunk the brew, fearful that has I had damaged my brain, I felt mentally broken down. I called out to Liam who held me and caressed me with words of hope and courage.

After the ordeal was over, I eased into recovery. During the integration mode, unlike the previous trips, this time I got flashbacks for weeks after the session, it took a couple of months to fully recover. Liam sustained the healing process, and I eventually became free. This was my last session, and the process was completed, the desire to do it again never came back. The guides announced I had accomplished my work with the plant medicine.

Still today I am perplexed about how on Earth I volunteered to repeat such an experience. 'What was I thinking? Why would anyone repeat such torment?' How did the memory of the trauma vanish every time? My experience with the plant spirit was very bespoke, unknowingly I had united with an energy healer to clear ancestral roots. A deep cleansing had taken place my Crown Chakra had undergone an intense reprogramming. I had upgraded myself in the process with new programming, I had been rewired and a new me had emerged. Contentment in my life became clear, my financial situation stabilised, direct access to my higher self, amplified I felt brave, stable, and secure.

Following my last session, I was never drawn to repeat another trip on the plant medicine. Today the thought of it repels me. Whilst my aim was liberation and knowledge, many who use psychedelics may not have the same aim and may not undergo such an extreme experience. Nevertheless, I find it incomprehensible how anyone can consume psychedelics in a non-spiritual setting, my trips were extremely intense. I would never wish such an experience on anyone. I would therefore not recommend plant medicine without a safe environment or a skilled practitioner closely supervising who also provides adequate aftercare, one never knows what the plant spirit has in store for you.

We will move in and out of fear and every time we do, we will become more resilient until we let go of fear altogether then we will become free, I had unplugged and awakened without knowing it. Like a seed I had grown and transformed, so had the world around me. Now I could see both clearer, the dark and the light. The new light shining upon the world rich with information revealing the dark which could no longer hide. A veil hanging over me had lifted. There it was, clearer than ever.

Media Impact

'*A society built on lies is a prison. We build our own prisons when we give up our powers to think for ourselves, by expecting others to be responsible for our health*'

Our World is a theatre set up to seduce us into an acquiescence that dances to the tune of skilful marketeers who are also puppeteers to a hidden entity that disguises itself in various ways and controls the enterprises that rule the World. Our media, movie, music, art, fashion, and beauty industry are full of predictive programs that confine us to think the same and to live up to ideals dictated by a small minority that dominates the media with corrupt agendas. Playing on people's emotions prompting fear, with subconscious programming fed to us daily, promoting insecurity and anxiety while dictating the ideals we should chase after. When life does not reflect that ideal, many find their lives unsatisfactory or even worse fall into depression. When we become followers, our intuition is dimmed. It could not be more evident that the mainstream media, politicians, big pharma companies, public education authorities or religious leaders do not act in the best interests of the people. Yet only very few people speak out against them. It seems humanity has been turned into a species with amnesia, unable to acknowledge the manipulation that stares them right in the face. The media's prime purpose is to manipulate. They use all the tricks up their sleeve to program people to be the same, preventing the flourishing of their own authenticity.

We should all ask the question. Why is it that the media channels promote news that is predominately full of negative news and rarely celebrate the magnificence of humankind? Why do they promote violence over happiness or victimhood over self-empowerment? They could teach us alternative means that would contribute to our planet's wellbeing or make us self-sufficient and free instead of fostering dependency and materialism. Imagine how humanity would thrive if the news providers would report positive inspiring subjects instead. What on earth is happening with our media?

It seems that the ability of people to think for themselves has been paralysed by constant propaganda. The media has skilfully placed themselves as the ombudsman of the people, presenting themselves as the trusty distributors of information. They have geared up skilfully selling us false ideals, convincing people that they can buy their freedom through dictated statuses.

I consider ninety percent of what is streamed through our main media channels as fiction. The mass media is an operating system plotting to mind control humanity to confine everyone to a dictated ideal. People watch extreme violence for entertainment, promoted all around us through movies, video games and even children's shows. How on Earth has humanity fallen prey to this kind of entertainment? The mass media owners are not our governors. Yet they have taken control over the masses, and other public figures, using them as puppets to play out their games. One moment they are celebrated and idolised the next they are broken down and torn to pieces by our news channels.

Most people induce themselves daily with fear based engineered systems, cleverly planted with subliminal messaging that are promoted across all media channels, even triggering people to shut off if they hear certain words that suggest self-empowerment or free will. Fear mongering is a tactic of control used by the mass media as a brainwashing mechanism to influence the World

Listen to the lyrics of our bestselling artists, the majority echo drama and heartbreaks, vocalising desperation and sadness to the World. What has happened to art? There are some pretty dark displays gracing our most famous art gallery walls with the most disturbing subjects. Instead of feeling inspired or mesmerised by some of the most celebrated art exhibits, I cannot help but feel more like puking and gasping for fresh air, not my kind of entertainment. Yet the real phenomenon is that so many are willing to accept this as normal, and fearful to speak the truth. It is beyond my comprehension how this type of entertainment is considered acceptable. What kind of influence are we humans exposed to, what is this doing to our subconsciousness particularly of our young generation? Let's ponder that for a while, this is like permitting all forms of violence. One can find many published studies about how TV and negative media lead to aggressive behaviour, TV channels are saturated with acts of violence. This is a severely distorted form of entertainment.

It seems like we have vast amounts of choices of entertainment available at our fingertips, right? yet, one cannot help noticing that all main channels document the same news and all cinemas stream more or less the same movies. If one dares to look deeper, you will find that there is a tiny group of people that control the distribution of information through newspapers, publishing houses, news stations, the internet, video game developers, film productions, and other media channels. In 2000, there were six that were known as the big six, though only five dominate the industry in 2021, Time Warner, Disney, Murdoch's News Corporation, Bertelsmann of Germany, and Viacom.

It is tough to think creatively when one becomes a consumer of mass media programming. People who spend most of their free time in front of the television or peering at their smart phones listening to the radio playing in the background or falling asleep while the television or radio is running are spending huge chunks of their time being programmed. Programming the viewer when to laugh, cry, be angry, fearful, and to have all sorts of opinions about something or someone. Consciously or subconsciously, everything we see, hear, and surround ourselves with will influence us. The impact that this form of programming has on our decision making is enormous.

The Dark

But who are they? I have researched all legitimate organisations' names and then the secret societies that are behind them, only to find that behind them are further smaller secret groups, and then smaller ones behind them who will misuse their powers for as long as we participate. So, the vital question to ask is, not who they are, but at what point have we allowed ourselves to become like them and participate in their dark matrix games. All the religions and even our most famed new spiritual teachers have been created by them. Feeding us with part of the truth, yet something seemed to be missing, it lacked an authentic purpose.

Had we fallen for more massive brainwashing propaganda? What exactly was wrong with what these so called new 'spiritual teachers,' scientists and philosophers were feeding us about the Law of Attraction? They have given us all the techniques on how to attract all we desire into our life and told us to only look at what feels good. Admittingly, it had served me seemingly well, though at the same time something seemed off. Though what could possibly be wrong with that?

I like so many bought into this massive Law of Attraction campaign, which is a valid law, yet simultaneously we were being steered to create this protective bubble, so we can say we are feeling happy, life is fun, I am attracting lots of money to buy those shiny things and whenever there was something negative appearing in my experience, I should distract myself and look away, out of fear that I will attract more. Surely this could not represent the full truth. The truth must be deeper and more powerful than that.

Such an outlook is based on fear, creating a material dark world, the 3D Matrix, that has a grip on everyone and seems to be attractive to so many. Truth never resists anything, those who resist or become fearful are not in alignment with their pure powers.

'The ability, and extent that one can hold light is directly proportional to the ability to see the darkness.

What is the 3D Matrix?

A programming that keeps us plugged in a loop of consumerism, keeping us distracted from exploring our most potent authentic superpowers, it makes us lose sight of who we truly are. It is the agenda of those that rule, that do so much to keep us all logged into a programming embedded into us from early birth, it is fed to us daily via various repetitive coding that cleverly breeds inadequacy and fear, through culture, religion, movies, and mainstream media. It convinces us that we will never be or have enough, that some are better than others, that the planet has not enough resources, it tells us that time is linear and we are alone, and no other intelligent life exists in the universe. It suggests that our government has our best interest at heart, that humans need to be stifled and mind controlled to submission. It gets us hooked on alcohol, drugs, and unhealthy food, it spreads stress and anxiety which jeopardise our health. It drags us away from holistic healing, makes us lose our experiences of the present and sells us mindlessness instead of mindfulness, it aims to dim our own potent life force, our true frequency that would liberate the world.

Once we start questioning life, we realise that we live in a system that is flawed and corrupted and see the hitches. Initially we will want to resist the corrupt system, we will want to fight it and expose it. Though as our awakening proceeds and puts us on a path of accent, eventually we will remove ourselves from this system, which will lead this flawed system to crumble. Since we are the ones holding it in place, as we move towards liberation and towards truth, we will become a more refined divine version of ourselves.

'The Truth passes through three stages. First, it is ridiculed. Second, it is violently opposed. Third, it is accepted as being self-evident.' Marco Lopor.

Being subjected to the same kind of influences leads people to think along the same lines as everyone else, this disempowers us depriving us of independent thoughts. Even the education system is compromised, a structure where everyone is being taught to follow a predicted scheme that has been put in place by someone that decides the curriculum materials, limiting students' abilities depriving most from their potential to express their true talents. Leaving many students in debt before they even had a chance to evolve into their true potential. Our structure is keeping us so busy fending for our survival, feeding us with distracting headlines and leaving us with very little time to think.

Then we have Hollywood as merely another religion. Look at the worship of celebrities taking place, what are they doing that is so altruistic? Let's pause for a moment here and be diligent, what about your God given authenticity, what is this superior status that is being promoted? Could it be a distraction from your own capability to rise and shine, be discerning, though by all means do not let yourself get distracted with the comparison, that will catapult you straight down to a lower frequency.

How truthful can we be with ourselves? Transparency and authenticity are required to gain integrity. Will you dare to go beyond this propaganda? Those who do may notice that the majority are living someone else's dream instead of theirs. While all along the tabloids are taking care that we stay stuck right there, most people are programmed to undermine their own magnificence, groomed to toil the reality of someone else's celebrity status.

Programming

There are two awareness running our emotions, the false matrix programming and an authentic consciousness. So, when we direct our focus at the part of the truth that feels good, we look at certain things, and state, *'great this feels so good, let's keep our attention on this,'* which is all very well, though there will also be those moments when we become aware of something not so good. *'So, wait a minute, there is suffering over there, some rather dark things going on, animal cruelty or child abuse, or human trafficking, 'oh…no,no,no…' , this can't be true it doesn't feel good, let's not look there.'* This part of us feels threatened and falls into a state of horror when confronted with such terrifying events. In this state of fear, one does not dare to look, this fear based awareness is matrix programming diverting us from our divine core and power. In the matrix, our mind is not our own.

Our work must be to reclaim and enforce our sovereignty and keep our space clear of their programming. When we go into silence, unhindered by the stimulants of the matrix, to sit and be, for as long as it may take to reach that point of stillness, our true consciousness will fill our hearts with divine light and love, bypassing our matrix programming, once this happens, we reconnected to our true core, opening to the divine higher frequency that is available to us, and be amazed at the wisdom that comes forth to assist. Our authentic awareness, our divine Godlike core never excludes anything, it will not shy away from looking at all things because it is the whole truth, it will know and see all, it will never be fearful, it holds divine authority, every time we connect to our true heart, we let go of fear, this is how to achieve mastery. When we connect with our divine consciousness we become the masters, the true captains of our vessels and we shine our true light. We will then bring divine light to soothe and transform the darkest places.

Once we align and find this point, this however does not make us stay aligned forever more, it is a continuous process. Why? because we are constantly bombarded with the stimulants of the matrix programming. Yet with alignment to our higher source energy, we will remember that the power lies within us, this will help us raise our frequency and move us collectively beyond this matrix programming. It is crucial to stay focused which will move us into liberation, carrying us beyond our greatest fears.

No one is born to operate under someone else's agenda, those who do are surrendering their dreams. Every being on this planet has something about themselves that is spectacular in its unconventionality. We took birth to express ourselves through our true essence, we were not born incomplete, neither were we preconditioned to seek out someone to complete us or wait for validation from society. When we give ourselves the space to nurture our individuality, we will automatically allow everyone else to do the same. We have all we need inside of us, and those who are fortunate enough to walk with us explore with us and discover our uniqueness are in for the best ride of their life. Imagine a world where everyone is free to live up to their potential to explore their unique gifts. Envisage the satisfaction we would find in marvelling at each other's genius.

All there is genuinely left to do is to break down those programmed belief patterns we have been fed with and in the process, we will awaken to the fact that our universe is indeed a free will zone yielding to us the magical life that we came to live. Once we refrain from worshipping false idols and align with our higher source we will fall in love with our life then no media influence can manipulate our minds.

Telepathy or Mystic?

I have always had a fondness for uncommon people. Relationships kindled by an unusual encounter. During my early years of being a BK, Edric suddenly appeared on my computer screen, unannounced. A friend who was helping me to resolve an issue with my computer had introduced me to one of his acquaintances, it was Edric who was an expert in computer science.

We first chatted via video messenger. He generously offered his help and took over my computer remotely and fixed the error in minutes. Edric had the most amusing sense of humour, blunt but with a blithe nature. He introduced himself as a Luxembourg Lord living in the Canary Islands. Edric was charming in a very mercurial way, which delighted me. Almost daily he would, confess his undying love for me. Although We had an instant connection, I was deeply involved in my spiritual studies at that time, and not easily swept off my feet. I was pleasingly committed to my BK disciplines which could not be trumped. My communication with Edric felt safe as he lived in a different country, and we communicated via messenger.

Edric was one of the few non BK people I knew who practised meditation. We chatted daily about the most intriguing subjects. Our conversations were adventurous, we exchanged spiritual mysteries and enjoyed playing competitive mind games. We often experimented with telepathic messaging and would try to read each other's minds, our exchange was playful. I discovered many secrets about Edric which I did not grasp fully at the time. His meditation practice was part of a Freemason tradition, and he later explained that he was also one of the order's highest ranking members. I remember his profile picture kept changing to the eye of the Pyramid. At the time I did know the meaning of the symbol or the purpose of such a society and I was not particularly interested in it.

Edric was considered a genius in his field. A brilliant mind with an adventurous nature. He had at the age of fourteen as part of a rebellious group hacked into forbidden security data codes. As a result, he had been banned from various countries and was retained to provide his services to a government body in exchange for release from a prison for juveniles. Although he was an adult by the time I met him with his hacking times supposedly over he was still unable to enter the UK, his long ban was lifted a couple of years later.

Edric would often be in my mind, in the real sense. He popped in and out of my life over the next ten years, he kept in touch via instant messaging and telepathically and we met on occasions after his ban had been lifted. The connection we initially established had felt exciting, though as years passed, his unpredictability became restricting I felt his influence when I did not desire it, without realising I had given way and had allowed him to pierce my protective energy field. Edric was tall, his appearance handsome. He had become a father and was divorced shortly after. He entered affairs with various movie stars, a subject he liked to talk about, yet his stories were full of heartbreaks and quarrels.

Edric had multi personalities, one side of his personality was delightful whilst the other felt destructive and manipulative. Edric had no lines on the palm of his hands. His story about his birth was a rather peculiar one, he described his birth, as I today understand it to be a 'walk in,' meaning his soul joined an existing body of a young boy of around ten years of age. He was not born on Earth through the womb. When I questioned him about it, he further described the boy he joined as a nasty boy, according to him no pictures of his childhood exist. He never fully explained his story, and whenever I questioned him further, he had a way of redirecting me to avoid the subject.

He also mentioned underground cities and tunnels that he had visited which existed in various countries. To take it a step further he also stated that he had drunk blood and tasted human flesh whilst he made fun of my vegan lifestyle. I laughed it off in disbelief. How could such a thing be true? My reaction amused him and I dismissed his story as a tease. On a different occasion Edric spoke of the children, the innocent children and the paedophile rings he had dedicated himself to expose. Again, when I questioned him further, he dismissed me, yet I could see a disturbing pain in his eyes.

Edric seemed well trained in harbouring his telepathic powers. He was a skilful mind manipulator. I often felt trapped by his influence, unaware it led me to be drawn into a lower frequency field that felt depleting, robbing me of my life force. I was not fond of this experience. The more I tried to move away, the more I felt captured. It took me a while to notice that I was being mentally manipulated. I often argued with Edric demanding that he disconnects, and he seemed to be amused that I had figured it out.

It took me years to recognise how unwanted invisible influences can feed on the life force of others. As I was learning about vibration I knew how to draw in divine light and stabilised this new higher frequency range as a part of me. As I did Edric was naturally thrown out of my vicinity, he could not intrude and was unable to sap anymore.

Edric evaporated out of my life appearing occasionally on the scene, and when he did it was an indication for me that I had to step up my frequency range. Beings that feed on our divine life force are closer than we think, they can obtain access when we open up to them feel low or during moments of anxiety. Vibrational tuning is our true protection and very worthwhile practising.

The Grand Awakening

The idea that spirituality had to be a certain way had faltered. All those images of enlightened masters granting light and blessings to worshipping crowds, and saints with their halos, kneeling in prayer, appeared like images that demanded compliance instead of truth. Certainly, an implausible projection of what I considered an awakened state of consciousness. I have outgrown those allegories, the notion that I had to rely on something outside of me to aid my spiritual evolution perpetuated a separation from my connection to my higher self. Why would anyone need to attempt to become enlightened or God like? I do not believe we need to follow doctrines or examine our conscience to see if we are worthy of love, a truthful God equals love, all it takes is to simply ask for love and let Source light in and let God become you.

I had glimpses of myself as a multidimensional being with a galactic heritage and with it emerged a full history of many existences I lived. While here on Earth, I had faced my share of challenges, the pain of loss, betrayals and disappointments but also, I had learned about the riches, laughter, love, and joys of life. Any trauma I had experienced was with the heart breaking belief that I was alone, rejected and abandoned. I have lived with many highs and lows, it was the call to the truth that was calling aloud like a siren.

The truth is unstoppable, when one's frequency rises the grains of truth will reveal themselves all around. I had to continually adjust to learn how to let go of old dysfunctional patterns, relationships that no longer worked, and identities that no longer fitted. It felt like I was undergoing a deep cellular memory clearing. Looking back at my life I could see that everything I had been doing was a step by step cleaning up process, anything that was dense or negative that I held within my cells was purging out.

I entered a challenging matrix system altering consciousness on a collective assignment, as I was clearing up dense energies within myself, I was also supporting the Earth's collective awakening, clearing out ancestral lineages, shedding layers of toxic beliefs and long held emotions. While doing all this, I was awakening to spiritual energies that lay beyond my human imagination. I witnessed others raising their frequencies also awakening to the truth, the collective was aligning. The light was shining into the dark leaving no tolerance for falsehood anymore, so many are now starting to see through the deception we have lived, all is being disclosed. Earth is being cleansed. It is on its way to a frequency change, it may seem that things are getting worse though everything we are observing was always there, what is occurring is that the veil of amnesia is being lifted, and the truth is being revealed for all of us to see. When we as a collective come together, demanding the truth, love, and peace, we will step into our powers. Our positive belief pattern will raise frequency, causing a ripple effect that will then automatically be accepted vibrationally expanding wider into our society, to reach a critical mass. It is this that will create the desired collective shift, this phenomenon is known as the 'hundred monkey effect'.

Our planet is in the midst of the greatest awakening. Waves of light are being projected through the Sun from higher realms to be anchored into the Earth's grid. These higher vibrational forms assist the collective to raise frequency and support the stabilisation of a multidimensional grid of a benevolent order. As the high frequency light anchors into the Earth, it will purge the darkness. This shows up as the chaos and deception we are now seeing play out on Earth. These high frequency spikes also show up on the Schumann Resonance chart. As we become a link within this upgrade our energetic field will likewise undergo a magnetic upgrade. Our bodies are being recalibrated into our natural multidimensional state, our human physical apparatus that is made from cells, the pineal gland, neuronal junction, spinal fluid are being upgraded electrically. We are becoming ready for a monumental shift, the era of fear and survival is coming to an end, and this ending brings a new beginning. This shift in consciousness will change our government, financial system, and environment. As we raise our frequency, we are slowly withdrawing our attention from this dysfunctional dense third dimensional frequency reality, into a magnificent new world. A place where poverty and illnesses are eliminated, to an abundant planet that holds riches of wildlife with outstanding reserves where nature thrives peacefully. Gaia the soul of Earth is now moving from the third dimension into the fifth. All souls on Earth can ascend to make this shift into the fifth dimensions. As the collective consciousness rises, we will start to remember who we are. As we expand, we make our way back to sublime divinity to the highest form of intelligence. To expand we must also make peace with the malevolent existence and then dissolve this part of our soul. We will be faced with many incidents we may judge as merciless, but judgement will not serve us. We must hold firm to the remembrance that we are in a free will zone and a Divine Plan is in place to free this planet, this is the last plan, and the last card to be played is going to be an Ace.

Deprogram Those Bedtime Stories

Those thoughts that were embedded into my mind, from stories we all listened to as children. Waiting for a knight in shining armour riding a white horse who always came to the rescue. Undoubtedly a belief that had to be broken down in my reality, this is not the kind of rescue I desire, no rescue is needed, we are our own liberators, there is only one saviour and that is oneself.

It feels easy to adopt the victim mentality at our most vulnerable moments. Believing that someone outside of me will fix all my problems, or some universal force will land in my back garden and save the world. While such thoughts can be entertaining and may even allow a moment of hope, they can quickly turn into false thoughts of hope that run randomly in our minds holding us back from taking the necessary steps to become free. There is only conscious or unconscious participation, being on autopilot and letting our thoughts run wild or constantly reliving memories, these are of no benefit.

This unconscious mental trap is far from the happiness most of us seek. The decoding of the old paradigm of female victimhood starts when we as individuals and collectively ask for the freedom we desire. Most humans do not know how to express their deepest needs. Instead they put up with misery not knowing how to find the way out, living this cycle repeatedly, often believing external forces will fix things when it is the inside that needs healing. Liberation is key and one must persist and ask for guidance on how to find the way out, only then can all the love, safety, beauty and riches of life unfold.

Women have been undermined for years, their expression and greatness suppressed by social systems in which men dominated the authorities and social privilege. Though the world is moving into a time of awakening where such unjust privileges are being dismantled, and feminine energy is prevailing, not to be superior, but rising back to its fullness. It is a time to rise and to let go of any engagements with lower vibrational energies. The feminine energy has been preparing in strength and love and will also assist the masculine energy to find his way back to the light, for the unity of the female and male.

Without doubt I noticed that our capable, strong, free of addiction and independent men have somehow dispersed in our society. The matrix has been hard at work brainwashing many of our men to become obsessive over pornography or turn them into obedient transgenders. Promoted by the fashion industry and through art letting the compliant betas lead and muting the alpha manhood. These men have forgotten their God given powers and their masculine cosmic roles and family bond.

A time of healing is required for the wounds of the female and the male, both have been shaken out of balance, the recovery is taking place as the feminine collective is shifting out of the fear mentality into a new space of strength and divine love.

Great changes are taking place on the planet, like never before, women's strength is sprouting, emerging from all corners of the world. This is a great time to be alive and to drop all forms of victim mentality. We are continually moving in an ever expanding upward spiral without end, there is always another timeline to explore, another life to live, new talents to master.

Our light is growing brighter, blending in for the benefits of everyone, this quiet power has landed. It is the time to level up and never again allow ourselves to remain exposed to anyone or anything that feels unkind or unloving.

A Power Called Light Language

Light is a frequency that carries knowledge. When we listen to or read higher knowledge or sounds, we also receive the embedded coding that is transmitted with it triggering our consciousness to expand. This can be through high frequency music, tonal vibrations, or visuals. When our consciousness expands, we unleash extraordinary talents.

It was the summer of 2019 and prodigious changes transpired during my meditation practices. I observed the muscular pulsations that I felt during deep states of meditation become more and more predominant. Some gentle energy was guiding my facial structure into detailed movements. My nose, cheeks, and lips twisted and wiggled. My mouth opened wide, compelling me to stretch out my tongue. I was taken through precise facial moves, but it was not me conducting them. Then the tones started to come through, I stopped in between as I had to laugh, I had no clue what was going on, while I kept control over my body, something was exercising my facial structure and my vocal range. Words started to form, perfectly shaped syllables were echoing through my mouth, which took the shape of a language I had never heard nor could understand. At that point, I realised that I was transmitting or channelling a form of energy. The experience felt uplifting and exciting. I started asking questions, 'who are you?' the word *Sha…man* followed by the word broken up and repeated Plei…ad..ian. I continued asking, 'what is your name?' a word that sounded like Hajumiti transmitted. 'Are you able to speak in English?' I enquired, and I received the answer: *'I am you, you are me.'*

The transmission continued with singing and humming of various tunes. Some sounded like chants, I was not accustomed to chanting. My body was gently guided to perform a series of automatic breathing rhythms, and I was able to hold my breath for a very long time. I spoke and sang in tones that sounded like a mix of Japanese and Finnish. My bodily organs were being fine-tuned, my vocal and facial muscles were being exercised. I was curious to understand the purpose and meaning of this. I was aware that Sha…man (Shaman) translates into healer.

I suspected the words that I was transmitting could be an extra-terrestrial Pleiadean language. At this time, I still had very little knowledge of the existence of extra-terrestrials. I started my investigation and my research led me to various people who were well versed in this subject and had direct telepathic access to the Pleiadian and the Hathor's extradimensional consciousnesses. I learned that the sounds I was transmitting were light codes known as Light Language. As my discoveries unfolded, I received two personal messages over five months directly from the Pleiadian and following those two further messages from the Hathor's that introduce themselves as ninth dimensional consciousness.

I had acquired a substantial upgrade, that triggered my memory of stored knowledge, from a different level of my existence, outside of this Earth's matrix. I learned that the soul aspect of myself known as Ivana on Earth is closely aligned with an element that is Pleiadian, from a central civilisation star known as Taygeta, that has a planetary mainstay known as Heioanae, and this star was my soul home. The spontaneous fluid body movements I was experiencing turned out to be known as Kriyas, which are orchestrated by my higher self and served to prompt me to a higher activation.

The Pleiadian and the Hathor's were focusing waves of celestial light energy that I was able to receive and transmute into tones known as Light Language. The frequency of the Light Language entails a coding that projects a high vibrational frequency signal reaching deeply into the DNA. As I was prompted to vocalise them it felt uplifting and deeply soothing. The light codes that were being transmitted were carriers of divine frequency to awake dormant abilities. Light is a carrier of frequency that holds information. The projected tones unlock energy doorways that change our perceptions, basically with this change in our perceptions healing can take place.

I was able to use the language with the intention of releasing energy that has been stored or trapped plus merging myself with it at various vibratory rates. The Light Language amazed me I practised it daily and used it to assist people with emotional healing.

So how does it work? The Light Language is not a language as such but impulses of Source light that transmit through my body. The light frequencies form tones that sound like a language. Initially I did not understand truly what was occurring, I had to research deeper into the subject of frequency rays and found that rays of gamma light can change the DNA of a living being. We are beings that are shaped by our universal history that consists of light coded filaments.

This Earth plane is subject to a system that has a limited light frequency which subdues self-empowerment, and the extraordinary talents that everyone possesses. Currently we humans only have two DNA strands activated, and more strands lie dormant which science refers to as junk DNA. The more DNA strands that are active, the more progressive the consciousness of the human being. Once the dormant twelve DNA strands are activated the full use of our brain will be accessible and we will remember who we truly are.

Energy takes many forms, light codes that transmute as Light Language activate the dormant DNA strands, light carries knowledge, naturally transmitting electromagnetic waves of consciousness that hold knowledge, those sound frequencies impulse deeply into the listener rearranging the light coded filaments of the human DNA, we are magnetically and biogenetically tuned. We are multidimensional beings born on earth without full conscious memory of who we are elsewhere. We are masters in the process of awakening, through the encoding of dormant DNA.

Everything is energy, sound is energy, experiences and memories are forms of energies. Our cells store and hold energy and experiences of past and present lives. These experiences may have been pleasing and joyful and some may even be terrifying. Old energies remain alive affecting our personality and life choices until cleared through conscious Intention.

Remembering Who We Are

'That version of me, the people of my past know is a version of me that doesn't exist anymore'

The greatest technology hidden from humanity is our own consciousness. An extra-terrestrial is the upgraded version of ourselves. Universal truth makes itself known once we seek it, and when it does, it will show us that there is no authority above anyone. It will show us our beauty enabling us to recognise ourselves as a fragment of God, an infinite and sovereign inhabitant of the universe.

We know our world consists of many races and cultures. If our Universe is unlimited and we know it is. It must logically follow that multi universal races exist that inhabit many different solar systems and planets with diverse vibrational frequencies allowing a soul to have all sorts of living experiences. The Universe has many civilisations, some are benevolent, and some are malevolent. Civilisations that vibrate above the fifth dimension are benevolent and highly intelligent and far more advanced than humanity. Now we may question, *'Why would I need to know all of this since I am stuck here in this lower dimension, would it be better not knowing. Is ignorance not bliss? Those that are asleep to it all seem to go about life unbothered?'*

As we ascend, we transform to high frequency beings and we will learn all of the truth, and go beyond fear. The 'Ascension energies' or 'solar flares' reaching earth are galactic light codes, that touch everyone to assist with this transformation. This is information from a high consciousness that is being anchored into humans' subconscious, this information is going to nurture humanity. It will serve to guide and expand consciousness. But like seeds, it is not known how each will grow, but we must trust the growth, and continue to nurture these seeds with love and joy, and they will grow.

Knowledge will always serve us. The people who are awake and aware are the ones that have a much easier ride due to their understanding and their ability to create consciously and alter their realities from negative to positive. It serves us to know that the malevolent exist, as they are merged with our third and fourth dimension. It is of benefit to grasp how complex reality truly is. It may appear that the unaware are going about their business unbothered, although what is happening is that they are desperately clinging to an old reality that is crumbling. Eventually all will wake up as they witness the breakdown of this old reality.

Earth is a third dimensional planet with many limitations. We humans vibrate on a frequency so low that we have forgotten about our Godly powers. Every soul is given the opportunity to become free from the loop of low frequency incarnation. We must fine tune ourselves to evolve into higher consciousness. Fifth dimensional extra-terrestrials are highly evolved spiritual beings emanating unconditional love with magnificent light bodies who live on splendid planets. There are many benevolent races residing in different dimensions ranging from the fifth to the twelfth. The Pleiadian, Sirius, Arcturus, Orion, Hathor, Andromeda and Lyra/Vega. So called UFO sightings are nothing new. We now live in a time when many of us have witnessed advanced craft travelling through our skies and have made direct contact with our galactic brothers and sisters and have even been on board their incredible space crafts.

Geometric Universe

'Secret society controls the world, history is false and religion is a lie.'

We live in a geometric universe and have many magical ways that assist in generating matter. Crystals are one of them, they are alive and growing. Crystals grow according to the blueprint in their DNA, containing information that determines their shape and colour, they also have a blueprint of sacred geometric principles, one can see this universal geometry in natural crystal formations. Crystals are natural objects with an inner crystalline state of perfect balance. Each crystal contains a unique pattern which when it is precisely cut to its proper geometric form and the human mind enters into a relationship with its structural perfection the crystal extends and amplifies this emotion also magnifying thoughts and intentions. Crystals hold harmonious geometric forms in an order known as quasi periodic crystal, these quasi-periodic patterns can grow continuously and fill all available space resembling the tree of life.

Marcel Vogel was a research scientist with many patents who worked for IBM, he explored the unique characteristics and functions of crystals. Marcel Vogel utilised crystals to store life force energy and as amplifiers when working with faceted crystals, he noted that crystals can be used for healing purposes and that one can build a personal relationship with crystals. One can use them to anchor protective grids that enhance the space around us. The Crystal faceting can be amplified to transmit an increasingly coherent stream of energy to a subject.

Researchers found that ancient Egypt had a power supply generated by crystals. We know that quartz crystals conduct electricity and keep highly accurate time in our watches. They are also used in LCD screens and LEDs. Silicon crystals are the heart of computer technology, It is notable that many natural minerals are used in advanced technology.

The ancient Egyptian pyramids are one of the World's most famous mysteries and there are also lesser known pyramids found on almost every continent perfectly aligned and strategically positioned. Researchers have found several thousand pyramids dotted around the globe. Using a high-tech aerial mapping technology, a team of archaeologists from Europe, US and Guatemala found thousands of ancient structures including pyramids in the dense jungle of Guatemala's Peten region, they also identified agricultural fields and water canals where around ten million Mayan people may have once lived within the area known as the "Maya Lowlands."

By using a mapping method named LIDAR, which stands for Light Detection and Ranging, a remote aerial laser light device that when aimed at the ground it reveals shapes and structures hidden by dense trees and plants. By using this method many pyramids have been discovered around the globe some on land buried or overgrown and others are disguised as mountains with visible outlines and some have been found underwater. More astonishing is that over 200 pyramids are scattered throughout Britain and Ireland of all sizes and ages. The structure of an Egyptian pyramid has exact geometrical dimensions precisely built with an orientation towards the astronomical or cosmic north and constructed according to the Earth's motions.

According to engineer, author, and researcher Christopher Dunn, the geometry of these ancient pyramids appears to serve harmonisation of the Earth's energy grid. Dunn points to the unusual interior design of the great pyramids and debunks the tomb theory. He states that no original mummies were ever found in any of the pyramids and that the claim by archaeologists that pyramids were built by slaves hauling stone blocks on wooden rollers is mathematically futile. As well as Dunn's findings, *Paulina Zelitsky*, a sea explorer, who has extensively researched the subject discovered pyramids under the sea and Dr Semir Osmanagich who identified colossal pyramids in Bosnia, also came to similar conclusions in the field of pyramid research.

The pyramids are built with rocks that have a high crystalline compound, ancient scripture depicts them as amplifiers to tune into the higher dimension and as generators of free energy. Authors, Erich von Daniken and Matias de Stefano, who is able to remember his past life, support the idea that the creators of the pyramids were extra-terrestrial engineers and scientists with advanced tools and technology. The thousands of pyramids that are so perfectly aligned and strategically positioned across the globe are a big network of computers connected to the cosmos. Whilst they have been dormant. The seven great pyramids are giant powerful cosmic computers that are programmed to awaken humanity and to activate the cosmic portal. This portal when opened will bring in the fifth dimensional light codes. The hidden pyramids of our planet that are so perfectly aligned are making themselves visible to us again. They play a significant role to help us shift into a much higher vibrational energy state. As the solar flares are hitting our planet the pyramids under the earth and the sea, and those on land get more and more activated, acting as amplifiers and the immensity of those energies will be felt by all beings.

Do It Now

'I have laughed, I have cried, I have triumphed, and I have fallen, all those components shaped me into something finer than before.'

Joy is the ingredient that makes everyone and everything beautiful. Bliss is beauty in its purest form, we are the most beautiful when we feel joyful. This emotion carries love, it is most attractive and carries a powerful vibration. This beautiful aura is not determined by body shape, hair colour or skin colour, but solely on how worthy and loved an individual feels about themselves. Love heals and makes us joyful and beautiful. One can only be as attractive as one feels, if you feel blissful then without doubt, you are at your most beautiful and become the catalyst that inspires the creation of beautiful things.

People are at their best when moving towards new experiences with purpose. We never stand still. Life always insists that we grow, expand, and become more than what we are. So many are afraid to be beautiful on the inside, the less we are influenced by others, the better. We must stand firm in our own authenticity with confidence. Our individuality and honesty are what makes us great beings. I count this type of beauty amongst the ultimate values of life.

'I had to maintain vigilance of who I was and who I wanted to become while moulding myself into the person of my dreams.'

I had exhausted the old me. It was time to grow out of myself and only look back to recognise that I am no longer the person I once was. I attended a thousand cremations of the various personalities I used to be, so that I could continually mould myself into an improved version of myself. The most valuable and best investment is in myself mastering how to apply myself. Every positive change I make to myself ripples outwards, it transforms the world around me.

Making time for myself has become immensely important. While this may seem selfish to some, it is the contrary, today I view selfishness differently. If I am not selfish enough to take time for myself and make improvements to my life, to reach my highest state of wellbeing then I won't have very much to offer others. The best thing I can do for others is to strive wholeheartedly to live my life through the power of example.

Those people that accuse others of selfishness and yet demand someone to change to satisfy their own needs should sincerely question who is really being selfish. I had moments in my life when I believed I could make someone change only to find that I am not able to turn anyone around, nor could I change my past. Yet I can create time and develop my own state of wellbeing. This is indeed an empowering and beautiful thing to do and the only thing I have total control over. The moment I understood that I was the one in charge of my wellbeing, any desire to control circumstances or people around me vanished, instead I took steps toward creating a more solid better version of me. So that I not only have an abundance to give, but I also release everyone from the responsibilities to adapt to my needs. This is true freedom and love.

I have never stopped learning throughout my life, I love learning, acquiring new knowledge and skills. Newness is amazing, there is always more to know, to do or to be. Learning never ends. I find it very satisfying to learn about new scientific and spiritual discoveries, or to achieve something new in sport or dance techniques that keep my body flexible. I experiment with all sorts of new ideas and pick up things that I feel provide positive transformations.

This is when I feel that I live life to the fullest. Life is best lived in the moment. My life is now, this moment is my point of creation. This 'now' is responsible for how I feel in the next moment, which later becomes the now. Moment by moment is the now, and indeed there is only one moment now. There is nothing more important than the now, and unless I change now, nothing will change. So, the now creates my future, and my future is now. Therefore, my current thoughts and feelings shape my future experiences, so my work must be done now.

Intuition

'When there is nothing left to rely on, the only thing left to do is to rely on oneself.'

We are all intuitive beings with an integrated guidance system, which lets us know if we are moving towards our wellbeing or away from it. This guidance system is called emotion. Emotions act as a system of navigation, telling us if we are on course or off course. Our integrated guidance system also tells us whether what we are told is the truth or not, for anyone that stands for truth, untruth will go against the grain. Anything that does not feel like freedom, love, joy, appreciation, knowledge, or empowerment indicates that we are off course.

Many people have lost the ability to read their intuition, so many are afraid to think for themselves. Intuition is feeling combined with logic, that would naturally be practised if one does not just blindly follow what an authority dictates or a celebrity figure promotes.

As a young girl, I grew very fond of the Sherlock Holmes and Miss Marple series. I was fascinated by those fictional characters. To the viewer, it seemed like they had superpowers. Their superpower was an excellent intuition and an ability to absorb details around them. Arthur Conan Doyle and Agatha Christie who created those characters must have had it figured out.

One can quickly determine the characteristics of a person by merely observing how they handle themselves. It is straightforward to figure out how for example your newfound partnership will eventually end up treating you. Even though a newfound engagement may seem all rosy at the first encounter, figuring out to what extent you can trust someone or the kind of partnership this will develop into a few months or years down the line is rather easy to determine. Look out for how your newfound friends or partners treat others, their family, belongings and how they interact in business. Observe how this person treats strangers, children and animals, do they care for the environment, are they attending to tasks that are exploitative to gain the most without care for others, or are they taking steps towards honourable activities that are sustainable and beneficial for many?

I have noticed that people that are messy and disorganised have similar thinking patterns, their thoughts are scattered and they are often unable to make focussed decisions. The partner or friend who continuously criticises others in your circle of acquaintances, you can be assured will speak in the same way about you when you are not present. Behaviour patterns are thoughts that remain consistent in someone's life. It is called the character or personality of a person and unless it is broken down and replaced with another behaviour pattern, It will persist through personal or business matters.

There is an order to how our emotion drives us, a neat explanation is to view them on an 'Emotional Scale,' it describes in sequence the scale of how our feelings are linked one following another. The scale commences from our highest vibrational feeling, which is joy and liberty to our lowest which is powerlessness. Each emotion is linked to another that either spirals us upwards or downwards.

As a BK, I was taught not to express any negative emotions, like sadness or anger, as it would reinforce undesirable thought patterns. A contrary version I also heard about was anger management where people were encouraged to let go of negative emotions instead, by expressing anger. I wondered why there were so many contradictory explanations. Until I stumbled on to these elucidations: 'The Emotional Scale,' by Abraham Hicks and the 'Map of Consciousness' by Dr David R. Hawkins, M.D., PH.D. which appears in his fascinating book, 'Truth vs Falsehood,' which outlines how consciousness is energy. The 'Map of Consciousness' presents the full range of emotions, from the most positive to the most negative.

To document his works, Dr Hawkins relied on a technique called 'Kinesiology' known as muscle testing, his research has been validated and published. I found his findings to be one of the most enlightened, a useful tool to assist me to understand and measure my emotions, where I was at, and how I would move forwards or drop back.

All those scattered emotions I had experienced suddenly made more sense. I was able to organise them. I drew up the below emotional spiralled scale to help me to understand my emotions better. Positive emotions help us to manoeuvre our way to sovereignty while following negative emotions disempower us. Personally, I experienced that it is necessary to express feelings such as sadness or anger rather than suppress them. However, as I learned it depends where one stands on the emotional scale. For example, if one feels depressed which equals powerlessness the next better feeling emotion would be revenge, from there to anger progressing to discouragement then blame, worry etcetera constantly moving up the scale. As anger feels better than revenge, discouragement feels better than anger and so on. What one does not want to do is to get trapped in any of the undesirable emotions or to spiral backwards into powerlessness. The key is to dive into every emotion, feel it and release it, whilst constantly moving up the frequency scale, to the next better feeling. Eventually reaching appreciation, empowerment, love, joy and freedom.

Consciousness is the energy of our emotion that creates our reality which reacts to the frequencies we emit. A higher consciousness operates differently than a lower consciousness. When we move into a community of higher consciousness, we will have a society with very little or no crime. There will be more freedom and more creative expression.

We have our individual frequency, as a community we also have a collective frequency. Frequency is measurable, humanity on this planet is currently moving through the vibration of courage, which means the darkness gets exposed, this is the time we are currently in. We are moving out of the third dimension into grander frequencies. The consciousness of courage means we have reached a level of truth and with truth comes the power of the fourth dimension.

'But how did humanity move into this vibration?' One may ask. You will find that it takes only fifteen percent of the population to move the whole collective into a new more benevolent state of consciousness. The elevated vibration of those fifteen percent spurs the rest of human consciousness with them. This is why your vibration is immensely important, because YOU, yes YOU, can affect the consciousness of the whole world. You are this powerful.

Freedom

Love

Appreciation Joy Knowledge

Empowerment

Passion

Enthusiasm Happiness

Belief

Optimism Hopefulness

Boredom

Pessimism

Frustration

Overwhelmingness

Disappointment

Doubt

Worry Blame

Discouragement

Anger

Revenge

Hatred

Jealousy

Insecurity Guilt

Unworthiness

Fear Grief

Depression

Despair

Powerlessness

You Cannot Put a Filter on Frequency

Light is knowledge, and knowledge leads to truth. Truth has a frequency that is felt in the same manner as we feel the human pulse, one can pick up the frequency of any information that is being communicated. We all have intuition the ability to concentrate, tune in and ask for truth, this is how we develop telepathic skills. There is no hiding from someone who is tuned into truth, they can read another person's frequency like a book, each individual's energy is a source of information that makes itself known. We are beings of love, not violence. Because violence is promoted all around us, we must remember that our nature is to unite not to be combative.

'No one truly wins unless everybody wins. '

There can be no space in the world for those who command, control or perpetrate violence. Love can be challenging to give or receive, when self-love is not intact, we feel like we must obtain approval from others. Being my own best friend may not always be the easiest thing to do when I am comparing myself with so many around me. Every time I compare myself to others, I am harsh on myself, but when I compare myself with my own heart's desire then it is just between me and my inner being.

To truly love oneself can be the most arduous task to untangle. I was not aware I lacked self-love. There are those that judge self-love as arrogant yet is a fundamental piece of contentment and freedom. Whatever happens in one's life reflects the degree one loves oneself. My lover can only be as good as I feel about myself, I virtually used the relationships around me as a mirror to measure how much I love myself, and it did not always look like very much.

I started training myself unswervingly to like myself with all my imperfections. There are many tools one can use to do this, one I used is the *'The Mirror Technique,'* something I discovered first by reading *'The Magic of*

Believing,' this technique has been written about by many authors such as Louise Hays and Claude Bristol who wrote about it in 1948. *'The Mirror Technique,'* is a superb method, a simple idea of standing in front of a clean mirror looking deep into my eyes affirming by speaking to myself that I love myself and other positive emotions of what I want to feel and be. This powerful tool has been around for decades, great people of the past have used the mirror technique, to program their desires firmly in their minds. The trillion cells in our body respond to what we believe to be the truth. Beliefs are simply thoughts that we focus on when we are thinking.

How we feel is projected outwards and it cannot be tampered with. Being loved does not depend on anyone around us, to be truly loved I must feel love. Not out of duty or to avoid feeling miserable but because I am an extension of pure love, source energy, my higher self always loves me no matter where I am. My higher self is the divine Source, this omnipotent presence is a significant part of who I am. This infinite Source is the life power of all that exists and expresses itself through me and every one of us. We are all 'energy' fused to one another; we are all an extension of God which I also refer to as Source.

As a BK, I learned to believe what most religions teach, that God's benevolence is dependent upon my adherence to my spiritual disciplines and when I am observant I will be worthy of his love. Nothing could be further from the truth, everyone is loved and worthy of love, God finds me magnificent and adores me profoundly. There is an endless steady stream of love flowing through each one of us incessantly focused on our wellbeing. I cannot separate myself from my higher being though if I change course and turn myself away from accessing that love by expressing adverse comments or judgments about myself or others, believing that I am unloved or unworthy, circumstances will align according to how I feel about myself.

'I am loved because I love, and I love because I am love.'

There is nothing more selfless than taking the time to acquire the art of loving oneself. Anyone who does not like themselves will hold expectations for someone else or something else to fill this gap. Though no one will be able to fill anyone else's void for very long. When I know how to love myself, I have no void to fill but instead an abundance of love to share. We are all responsible for our own degree of love none of us is made to satisfy each other's voids.

You and I are powerful beings with direct access to fulfilling any emotion we desire, no matter what anyone thinks or feels about us. Unless I love myself, I have no love to give to anyone, the more I love myself the more love I have to offer. I am a lover, and if I were not loving, I would not be who I really am.

Earth Is a Living Being

Earth is a living planetary being, just as we are living human beings, yet we trample all over our planet. We allow authority figures to permit the cutting down of her forests causing damage to her plant life. Over exploiting the elements and minerals and abusing the animal kingdom as if they were not critical to our life. How did our oceans become the place where we dump rubbish which releases toxins into the water killing the coral and sea life? Why are we not protecting the air, our precious life force? It is being harmed and degraded every day by pollutants from many sources including ships, cars, aeroplanes, factories, power stations and more. When did we stop caring how we harvest and manage our crops? Why do we allow forest clearance with little ecological concern for the future. All this is because greed and financial profits are allowed to come before our planet. In the literal sense, what on Earth is going on? The vibrational violence and suffering made by those acts ripple throughout our world and manifest in people's lives.

Earth has a name and is alive, our planet is universally honoured and known as Mother Gaia. A pulsating living planet, beautiful, abundant, and rich, it has unlimited resources to offer. Gaia is a wonderous magnificent being that has given humanity a platform to enjoy its beauty and made herself available to support life but not to be exploited. Gaia and all that lives on her need the same amount of attention and love as humans do. Walk through life knowing this, access Gaia and her wondrous resources, walk barefoot on her unspoiled land, let her know you love her, use your bare skin to synchronise with her through the soil and elements. Gaia will induce you to connect with healing electrons through your feet or skin, providing your body with wonderful health benefits. Feel the core of Mother Earth and her releasing electrons drawing into your body neutralising any damaged frequencies, this union is a magnificent way of keeping healthy. I walk barefoot on grass or sandy beaches and lay on grassland and rocks with my bare skin touching, listening, feeling her pulse and making conscious contact with our planet Gaia, Mother Earth who loves us so very much.

Consume Light and You Shall Be Light

Many of us have read books that landed in our hands at just the right moment initiating major shifts in our personal experiences. These are not accidental moments we have been on our personal awakening path from the moment we took our first breath.

All that we have and are experiencing makes each soul unique, as we find our way It will become apparent that no one holds the whole truth, yet some souls are naturally more advanced than others. We are continuously guided, and as we advance to each stage there will be no going back as the Light remains within us for all time.

Up to 2012 earth was only vibrating third dimensionally the planet has since then gradually raised frequency and is heading towards a mass awakening. The awakening is when the soul starts to recognise that there is much more to our life than what is commonly believed. Earth is now being showered with a finer, purer vibration. The Starseeds or Lightworkers are the conscious souls on the front line of this awakening, who are anchoring the incoming light codes, these higher energies are called ascension energies providing access to unlimited creativity for the soul to expand and to ascend into more knowledge and new creative fields.

'The light codes that reach us are also our protection from the lower vibrations.'

Embrace the light and breathe it deeply in! it takes a strong 'Light Being' to be able to take in such large doses of knowledgeable light and hold it inside of the human body's cells.

Prior to 2012 ascension was only experienced at the time of death by those that had mastered a unique spiritual evolution. At that time the denseness of the third dimensional vibration did not provide an environment to achieve ascension within a physical body, but it has now become possible, and we can hold more light to attain mastery. There are many masters today able to walk amongst us who are opening portals to allow high energies of love to penetrate the planet. Many very special souls known as the Starseeds are incarnating now to assist in this evolution.

Starseeds are Lightworkers that have decided to come forth to awaken, to show the way, to live out our own learning rather than convert anyone. As we share our experience, rather than teach, we will notice that what people hear is not our words but our vibration, and our vibration reflects our intention. Dictating the path of another's journey is trying to be right, the way forward is to anchor the vibration of love within ourselves, we are awakeners not lecturers we will show by being in our own vibration, as we point towards knowledge.

Consume light and you shall be light, our vibration does the work for us. All we must do is be who we truly are, we can create art, dance, make music and find ways to laugh. The positive energies that you will absorb and carry will alter your aura, emanating from you an attractive serene vibration, that will be healing for many, many will feel it and will be drawn to you.

Starseeds that have chosen to take birth on Earth have a seed implanted in their subconscious mind and see through the deception. There are approximately four point five billion Starseeds on Earth, some currently still unawakened. All anchoring divine light to raise the frequency on Gaia to manifest the 5D timelines of a golden age as depicted in ancient writings. There have been five golden ages on this planet previously the first was named Angala, the second Petranium, third Mu, fourth Lemuria and the fifth Atlantis.

The current progression of accession has been ongoing since the fall of Atlantis. We are currently on track to reach the 5D vibration, It is expected that by the year 2032 humanity will have fully anchored the fifth dimensional consciousness. Since our reality shifts into higher consciousness all hospital procedures will become obsolete, all the hidden technologies will be made available to humanity, med bed technology to be one of them. The med beds can regrow organs using light spectrums and frequencies. Every city will have many med beds plus other healing chambers that are capable of healing and repairing DNA and also age regress our bodies by up to 30 years.

This will mark the beginning of a glorious new timeline, unprecedented peace and freedom accompanied by divine technologies that will provide clean and sustainable energy. Replicators will be in every household, a piece of advanced technology that will know how to reconstitute matter from pure energy. A machine the size of a microwave or larger that can create objects, such as nutritious meals, drinks, medication, garments, spare parts and building materials plus many other items that may be required, all at the press of a button. Replicators will also be able to recycle. You may have seen this in Star Trek and be tempted to dismiss it as fantasy though if one truly understands how matter is created, remember anything the mind can conceive can be manifested.

Today we already have a similar device, a less advanced machine, the 3D printing kit. It is a fine example that is also known as a replicator. It is a piece of technology that runs a printer software that produces 3D objects at an impressive speed, twenty years ago this would have been unimageable. Considering this it may not be that far off to have a more advanced Replicator manifested into our reality.

As our consciousness rises, we will move into this magnificent dimension, this transformation is expected to realise in this very lifetime, we will witness the obliteration of hunger and poverty. Humanity will return to being a highly developed civilisation as they were during the existence of Lemuria and Atlantis.

The citizens of this New Gaia will not be required to work for survival, the wisdom of life and death will be understood, and enjoyed, everyone will be free to learn and engage in activities of their choice. Taxes will be withdrawn, and a new trustworthy financial system will be founded that is based on gold. Each citizen will have access to free energy, and replication devices capable of producing anything one can imagine, from food to other required objects. The Earth will be unrecognisable compared to how it is today.

True talent and art will triumph again, artistic works would be highly valued and automatically protected, theft of copyright for example would vanish, since every piece of art created by an artist, architect or designer would carry the vibration of the creator, and would be identified based on this personal energetic signature. Invention or artistic creations could therefore not be hijacked.

Lions Awake Lions

It is said that the entrenched sleepy one cannot be awakened but will follow their own trail of evolution, a sheep is known to follow. Yet lions are awakened by lions as their blueprint will be triggered when they hear the calling of strength, self-empowerment, courage, truth, love and unity. The lions will rise, the lions of truth are awakening in huge numbers now, and those sleepy sheep will turn and follow what is more predominant, the awakened lions. That is how the sleepy sheep evolve into lions. I too was once a sleepy sheep until I followed the trail of a lion.

Once you start questioning your current reality, your DNA is activated and you are awakening. Welcome divine Starseed you are adored beyond measure, yes you who are reading these words. You are a divine master you have known far diverse experiences and have lived in other higher dimensions in which divine love was the true frequency field. You lowered your frequency to come forth through the birth canal to assist in this ascension process on earth. You are one who is here to anchor divine galactic light to raise the frequency of earth. You originate in the stars and have agreed to come here in these challenging times. Many others like you are incarnated like blossoms blown by the wind to all corners of the world. The energy of Gaia has been hijacked and the Starseeds are on track to liberate her inhabitants. Know that you came forth to do divine work and it is almost completed, have no doubt, we are succeeding.

And perhaps if living on Earth may have felt a little uncomfortable due to the denseness, when you feel like you do not belong here, and being here made you feel uneasy and often misunderstood, know now why. Do you remember now who you are? do you remember that you are a divine being who has experienced a multitude of adventures on timelines in other star systems? You are like beacons, transmitters of energy, absorbing the rays from your galactic family, the ones who deliver the galactic light codes to you, the ones who activate your DNA. Activation after activation you will remember more and more, you will soon know that you came forth and took birth on planet Earth to assist humanity. You carry within you dormant bundles of light that are coded in your DNA. And the next time you are watching a public announcement, that the military have seen objects in the sky that they could not account for, you will get confirmation of what you already knew to be true. You will come to remember and know that there is a bigger story to who you are, you are much more than this physical body who is living out a lifespan of a single life on a single planet. You will soon remember where you came from, and even how you were created to be the way you are now.

You had many incarnations, some glorious and some painful. You have reached a time to heal the wounds, and as you do you transform all the negative energies you have experienced, healing the world in the process. As you focus on shielding your consciousness from spurious frequencies you are awakening to your core beingness, through alignment, meditation, high frequency food and connection with nature. You are here to anchor the truth of divine light, to bring forth peace and freedom to Earth. As you master how to detach yourself from negativity and you anchor more and more peace into your lives you are anchoring the love into the energy grids of Gaia. Things are shifting rapidly now. So, keep the faith, be brave, evoke your strength, you are unique in your expression. Keep uncovering your soul gems for they will shift the equilibrium of the planet back towards the light.

With love Ivana.

Some names in this book have been changed to protect the privacy of individuals.